EVERY
School,
EVERY
Team,
EVERY
Classroom

District Leadership for Growing
Professional Learning Communities at Work[TM]

ROBERT EAKER & JANEL KEATING

Solution Tree | Press

a division of

Solution Tree

555 North Morton Street
Bloomington, IN 47404
800.733.6786 (toll free) / 812.336.7700
FAX: 812.336.7790
email: info@solution-tree.com
solution-tree.com

Visit **go.solution-tree.com/plcbooks** to download the reproducibles in this book.

Printed in the United States of America

15 14 13   2 3 4 5

Library of Congress Cataloging-in-Publication Data

Eaker, Robert E.

   Every school, every team, every classroom : district leadership for growing professional learning communities at work / Robert Eaker, Janel Keating.

       p. cm.

   Includes bibliographical references and index.

   ISBN 978-1-936765-09-6 (perfect bound) -- ISBN 978-1-936765-10-2 (library ed.) 1. School districts--United States--Administration. 2. Educational leadership--United States. 3. Professional learning communities--United States. I. Keating, Janel. II. Title.

   LB2817.3.E35 2012

                            2011033465

Solution Tree
Jeffrey C. Jones, CEO & President

Solution Tree Press
President: Douglas M. Rife
Publisher: Robert D. Clouse
Vice President of Production: Gretchen Knapp
Managing Production Editor: Caroline Wise
Proofreader: Sarah Payne-Mills
Cover Designer: Jenn Taylor
Text Designer: Rian Anderson

A major theme of this book is that we can create schools that are good enough for our own children. Since the inspiration for our work has come, to a great degree, from the dreams we have had for our own children, it is only fitting that we dedicate this book to them.

To Taylor Keating:

From the time you were a baby, you've instilled in me the desire and the relentless passion to create schools that would be good enough for you and your friends to attend. You've been my constant companion for every step of the journey to improve learning for the White River kids. You learned to walk in the hallway near my school office. You learned to ride your bike in the school parking lot. You learned to read and make friends in the classroom. You have motivated me! Being Taylor's mom is my best and most important job.

—Janel Keating

To Robin Eaker Lake and Carrie Eaker Kerley:

Every day I appreciate the fact that I have been blessed with two very wonderful daughters. Being your father and watching you grow up to become such amazing adults has been the singular highlight of my life. I am so proud of you. You continue to inspire and motivate me every single day, and I love you dearly!

—Robert Eaker

Acknowledgments

We are grateful to Tom Lockyer, the superintendent of the White River School District, and the White River Board of Education for their leadership and support in the implementation of professional learning community practices within the district. We also want to express our appreciation and admiration for the administrators and the faculty and staff of the White River School District for their passion, hard work, dedication, and professionalism.

We would also like to recognize the contributions and support of the Solution Tree family, and in particular, the chief executive officer of Solution Tree, Jeff Jones. From the Professional Learning Communities at Work™ Institutes, to a wide range of top-flight resources, to constant encouragement and support, Solution Tree has been a constant and consistent partner on our journey. Simply put, the resources and support from Solution Tree have been a huge factor in our districtwide reculturing efforts. And we would like to say a special thank-you to our editor, Gretchen Knapp. Her enthusiasm, graceful touch, professionalism, and attention to detail exponentially increased the quality of our book.

Visit **go.solution-tree.com/plcbooks**
to download the reproducibles in this book.

Table of Contents

Reproducible pages are in italics.

About the Authors

Robert Eaker, EdD, is a professor in the department of educational leadership at Middle Tennessee State University, where he also served as dean of the College of Education and later as interim executive vice president and provost. Dr. Eaker is a former fellow with the National Center for Effective Schools Research and Development, and in 1986 was recognized by the *Phi Delta Kappan* as one of North America's leaders in translating research into practice.

He has written widely on the issues of effective teaching, effective schools, helping teachers use research findings, and high expectations for student achievement, and he has coauthored with Richard and Rebecca DuFour numerous books and other resources on the topic of reculturing schools and school districts into professional learning communities (PLCs).

In 1998, Dr. Eaker was recognized by the governor of Tennessee as the recipient of Tennessee's Outstanding Achievement Award. Also in 1998, the Tennessee House of Representatives passed a proclamation recognizing him for his dedication and commitment to the field of education. In 2003, Dr. Eaker was selected by the Middle Tennessee State University Student Government Association to receive the Womack Distinguished Faculty Award.

For four decades, Dr. Eaker has served as a consultant to school districts throughout North America and has been a frequent speaker at state, regional, and national meetings.

Janel Keating is deputy superintendent of the White River School District in Washington, where she ensures districtwide implementation of professional learning communities. An accomplished educator with more than twenty-five years of experience, Janel has served as an elementary and middle school teacher, elementary principal, and director of student learning. Janel first put PLC concepts into practice while principal of Mountain Meadow Elementary School in

Buckley, Washington. During her time there, Mountain Meadow was recognized as one of the highest academically performing elementary schools in the state.

Janel has been named Principal of the Year in Pierce County, Washington. She presents at state and national events, is a coauthor of *The Journey to Becoming a Professional Learning Community*, and has written numerous articles on leadership and school improvement. She coauthored with Robert Eaker the lead chapter in the 2012 Yearbook of the National Council of Teachers of Mathematics. Janel regularly consults with school districts throughout the United States. She is past president of the Washington State Association for Supervision and Curriculum Development.

Janel earned a master's degree in educational leadership from the University of Idaho and a bachelor's degree in elementary education from Carroll College in Helena, Montana. She received a superintendent's certificate from Seattle Pacific University.

Visit www.allthingsplc.info to learn more about Robert Eaker's work.

To book Robert Eaker or Janel Keating for professional development, contact pd@solution-tree.com.

Preface

Since the publication of *Professional Learning Communities at Work*™ (DuFour & Eaker, 1998) there has been heightened interest in shaping school cultures to reflect the professional learning community concept, leading to many different descriptions of what a professional learning community is, and what it is not, by a plethora of authors and practitioners. Many of these differences are small. Some, however, are significant and can have a huge impact on the efficacy of the PLC model to improve student achievement.

We want to be clear. The framework of this book is based on the professional learning community concept as described by DuFour and Eaker (1998) in *Professional Learning Communities at Work* and later revised in *Revisiting Professional Learning Communities at Work* (DuFour, DuFour, & Eaker, 2008).

The central word in *professional learning community* is *learning*. An intense and passionate focus on the learning of both students and adults is the cornerstone of the professional learning community framework, and one significant way in which we can learn is from the work of others. In particular, this book focuses on the work of the White River School District in Buckley, Washington, in the foothills of Mount Rainier. The district contains both rural and suburban areas, and since it's close to Seattle and Tacoma, increasingly it has taken on a more urban flair.

Although we have worked with numerous districts, we chose our work in White River as our exemplar for a number of reasons. White River has leaders who are knowledgeable, passionate, and relentless in their efforts to use PLC concepts and practices to improve schools and ensure more kids are learning more. The professional learning community concept was not one of a great many initiatives for improving adult practice and student learning, but rather *the* single initiative. This work was never optional; the district did not wait for everyone to buy in. They began their journey with passion and commitment, and they have demonstrated a willingness to stick with it.

Most important, White River's journey to become a model professional learning community has resulted in significant increases in student learning. A decade before becoming a PLC, student achievement in White River was lackluster at best, and in some schools, very low. During the five-year journey to embed professional learning community concepts and practices, student learning has increased across the district. By 2010, grades 3, 4, and 5 in White River had the highest math scores of the 15 districts and 126 elementary schools in Pierce County; math achievement in all of White River's elementary schools ranked near the top 10 percent in the state. In fact, Foothills Elementary School, which had been one of the lowest-performing schools in White River when the PLC journey began, rose to become the highest-performing elementary school in Puget Sound (of schools with an enrollment exceeding one hundred, in an area including two very large counties—Pierce County and King County). Foothills was also named a 2010 Washington State School of Distinction by the Center for Educational Effectiveness and the Washington State chapter of Phi Delta Kappa. Schools of Distinction include the 5 percent of schools that show the greatest improvement in the state of Washington.

Meanwhile, the graduation rate in 2007–2008, the year White River began districtwide implementation of the PLC concept, was 82.5 percent. By 2011, White River High School achieved an on-time graduation rate of 92 percent and had double-digit increases in science achievement, and 88 percent of the students at White River High School met or exceeded state standards for reading and writing. Nearly four hundred students enrolled in advanced placement (AP) classes (compared to just sixty students three years earlier). There have been significant increases in the achievement of students who traditionally performed in the bottom quartile.

District leaders in White River learned to ask fundamentally different questions as they implemented the professional learning community model. They no longer ask administrators, faculty, and staff if they "like" the PLC work, or if they "feel" this is a good way to improve learning. While they are sensitive to the perceptions and opinions of everyone throughout the district, the most fundamental question they ask is this: "Do we have evidence that the professional learning community concepts and practices are improving learning in the White River School District?" The data indicate an overwhelming yes!

We are often asked, "Can one school kick-start the reculturing of an entire district?" The answer is yes. In fact, this is often the case, and the White River School District is an excellent example. White River's journey to becoming a professional learning community began in 1998 when Janel became principal of Mountain Meadow Elementary School. Janel's daughter, Taylor, was eight months old at the time. Janel had the dream of creating an elementary school that would be good enough for Taylor to attend. Coincidentally, at the same time she became familiar with *Professional Learning Communities at Work* (DuFour & Eaker, 1998). Janel was determined to lead the reculturing of Mountain Meadow to become a model professional learning community, and these efforts resulted in significant increases in student achievement. By 2004, Mountain Meadow had become one of the highest-performing elementary schools in Washington State.

In 2006, Janel was named Deputy Superintendent for Teaching and Learning and charged with matching the success of Mountain Meadow across the district. In addition to reading books that Bob Eaker had coauthored on reculturing schools into professional learning communities, Janel had heard Bob speak at a number of Professional Learning Communities at Work Institutes and felt that Bob could be of assistance to the White River School District in its efforts to embed professional learning community concepts and practices. She reached out, and in 2006 Bob began to work closely with the superintendent, Janel, principals, and key faculty and staff. Bob became heavily engaged in the White River journey and along the way developed many deep and lasting friendships. In short, Bob has been adopted by the White River School District and has become a member of the district family. Since then, Bob and Janel have been regularly engaged in the hands-on, gritty work of reculturing an entire school district.

Embedding the professional learning concept throughout an entire school district requires, among other things, developing a deep, rich understanding of what a PLC is (and what it is not) and how it works—day in and day out. We realized early on that district leaders, principals, and faculty and staff were struggling to see how all the work they were being asked do fit together; they were having difficulty connecting the dots and seeing the big picture. To address this problem, we teamed with Rick and Becky DuFour to develop a roadmap, a graphic representation of the various stops a district or school must make on the journey to become a professional learning community. This visual resource, *The Journey to Becoming a Professional Learning Community* roadmap (Keating, Eaker, DuFour, & DuFour, 2008), was linked directly to *Learning by Doing* (DuFour, DuFour, Eaker, & Many, 2006) and ultimately to the work described in this book.

Implementing professional learning community concepts and practices has forced the White River School District to think and act in different ways. Working with district leaders, principals, and faculty and staff, we examined district practices and procedures ranging from how lessons are planned and learning is assessed, to how people are hired and mentored, to how progress on the journey to becoming a PLC is assessed. We've also worked to create a layered leadership structure in the district, with particular emphasis on the role of principals and team leaders. This layered leadership structure ensured that PLC concepts and practices would be deeply embedded in every school, team, and classroom within the district. We have highlighted and emphasized this *layered leadership* approach throughout this book.

As the efforts in White River began to positively affect student achievement, we began writing articles telling the White River story. And, as word spread about White River, leaders from other districts began to visit White River to observe first-hand the work of district office leaders, principals, and teacher teams. Districts from across the Northwest began asking for assistance in order to emulate White River's success.

As professional learning community practices began to take hold in White River, it became clear to us that if the district was to continue moving forward, district leaders would have to drill deeper into the work of a professional learning community, and that organizational structures, protocols, and forms would need to be developed in order to embed professional learning community practices deep into the district's culture.

Every PLC district must do work similar to our work in White River, and we believe that all districts, schools, teams, and classrooms can benefit from White River's experience. The resources and practical do-now strategies we developed there are the heart of *Every School, Every Team, Every Classroom*. We hope and believe the tools and experiences we share here can be valuable resources to others. It takes passion, persistence, and hard work to bring the power of the professional learning community concept to life across an entire school district, but the White River School District has demonstrated it can be done. This book is intended to share just how they did it! We believe there is much to learn from their journey, and it is our hope the experiences, practices, and resources from White River will make your own journey even more successful, worthwhile, and rewarding.

Introduction

This is a children's book. More accurately, this is a book about children and the kind of schools they need and deserve. Whose children are we writing about? Our children—yours, ours, our relatives', and those of our friends and neighbors. What kind of schools do we want for them? Schools where all students are safe, feel special, and learn at high levels—in every school, in every classroom, for their entire school career.

Every School, Every Team, Every Classroom is about the leadership that is required to create these schools. To make this happen, we desperately need a new way to lead schools. The fact is, there is a huge difference between *leading* the work of improving schools and simply *doing* the work of improving schools. *Doing* the work of improving schools implies routinely executing the tasks one is told need to be done in a rather mundane fashion—even if they are the right things to do. *Leading* the work of improving schools implies approaching the work with the passion and zeal of missionary! The reculturing of schools and school districts requires much more than completing a series of tasks. Improving schools requires leadership behaviors that motivate and inspire others to do things collectively that perhaps they never thought possible.

We believe the most effective framework for leading the work of schools is the professional learning community concept. We had one fundamental purpose for writing this book—to assist others who seek to *lead* the reculturing of schools and teams into true, high-performing professional

> *Improving schools requires leadership behaviors that motivate and inspire others to do things collectively that perhaps they never thought possible.*

learning communities in order to improve student learning. It is our hope that by sharing our experiences and what we have learned, we will help those who are undertaking a similar journey.

The Rise of the PLC Model

Since 2000, we have witnessed the rapid rise in the popularity of the professional learning community concept. Rarely in the history of American public education has there been such widespread agreement regarding the most promising path to school improvement. A broad array of researchers, writers, and practitioners has recognized the power of professional learning community concepts and practices to significantly improve schools (see DuFour et al., 2008, for a comprehensive discussion). Additionally, virtually every major educational organization has endorsed the core concepts and practices inherent in the professional learning community framework (see DuFour et al., 2008). Perhaps more important, schools and school districts across North America are reaping the benefits of professional learning community practices (allthingsplc, n.d.).

A New Understanding of District Leadership

Despite the emphasis on site-based school improvement that is inherent in the professional learning community concept, the central office can, and should, play a powerful role in enhancing the effectiveness of individual schools and teams.

Coinciding with this virtually universal recognition of the efficacy of the professional learning community concept, we have also seen increased attention on the critical role of district-level leadership in school improvement. In many ways, this is only common sense. If the capacity of teachers to improve student learning is enhanced by the school functioning as a true professional learning community, isn't it logical that the capacity of the *school* to impact student learning is enhanced when the entire district implements PLC concepts and practices? The answer is an obvious yes. Despite the emphasis on site-based school improvement that is inherent in the professional learning community concept, the central office can, and should, play a powerful role in enhancing the effectiveness of individual schools and teams. When schools and teams become more effective, in turn, classrooms become more effective in the work that matters most: ensuring student learning.

True District Reculturing

The excitement surrounding the idea of school districts functioning as professional learning communities is tempered by two hard facts. First, the vast majority of school districts (and schools) in North America maintain rather traditional school cultures. Second, we have observed that many school districts that claim to function as professional learning communities settle for *PLC lite*, randomly implementing a few PLC practices. In spite of the promise that the professional learning community concept offers for significant and sustainable school improvement, most school districts have failed to undertake the journey to actually becoming a professional learning community. A chasm lies between the endorsement of PLCs and the implementation of PLCs on a districtwide basis; some schools within a district may deeply embed professional learning community practices and significantly increase student learning, but others remain locked in the status quo. In short, many districts and schools adopt the *label* of a professional learning community, but few actually do the difficult, complex, and incremental work associated with deeply embedding PLC practices within the day-to-day structure and culture of every school, every team, and every classroom.

If there is virtually unanimous agreement regarding the power of the professional learning community concept, why haven't more school districts made the transition away from traditional culture? One reason is lack of a deep knowledge base. As we have worked with educators across North America, we've noticed many of them use the term *professional learning community* while in fact having only a cursory understanding of it. We concur with Michael Fullan (2005), who has observed that "terms travel easily . . . but the meaning of the underlying concept does not" (p. 67). Actually *becoming* a professional learning community requires a deep, rich understanding of professional learning community concepts and practices, coupled with the self-discipline and drive to embed professional learning community practices deep into district structures and culture.

Even when educators gain a deep and accurate understanding of the professional learning community concept, many simply do not know what to *do*—what steps to take. While there is no one way to becoming a professional learning community, there are certain specific *practices* that form the framework of the professional learning community concept. There are specific critical areas that must be addressed—stops along the way—if the journey is to be successful.

About This Book

This is not a book about defining what professional learning communities are or exploring the research base that supports professional learning community practices. Other excellent resources are available for those purposes (see, for example, DuFou et al., 2008; DuFour, DuFour, Eaker, & Many, 2010). Instead, this book describes how a district can actually implement the professional learning community concept and practices, using insights we've gained from experience working with educators across North America, particularly those within the White River School District, and sharing concrete examples of practices, resources, and tools that have been developed while doing this work.

While we believe the best way to learn how to reculture a district into a professional learning community is by doing the work, we find there is also merit in learning from the experiences of others who have successfully undertaken the journey. No two districts are alike, and every district will approach the journey in a different manner, but a basic tenet of a professional learning community is a commitment to seeking out best practice—learning from the experiences of others. We have had the privilege of assisting dozens of districts throughout the United States and Canada in their efforts to embed professional learning community practices and concepts. These districts range from very small rural districts to larger urban districts, from the Northwest to the Southeast. We've had the privilege of working with some of the most outstanding school leaders in North America. We have observed them in their work, and hopefully, we've also been of assistance to them. We have seen what they do and observed the effects of their leadership behavior and style. Most important, we have learned from them.

In *Every School, Every Team, Every Classroom*, we share what we have learned from these practitioners (using White River School District as the main exemplar). In short, this book is a description of how research, theory, and knowledge of best practice interface with the day-to-day work of school districts, schools, and teams that work to improve student learning in every classroom.

Chapter 1 explains the fundamental assumptions we hold about professional learning communities and the leadership behaviors that the rest of the book will explore. Chapter 2 examines how districts articulate and utilize the moral promise that lies at the heart of professional learning communities, and chapter 3 digs into how exactly district leadership builds the foundation of the PLC by creating shared knowledge. Chapter 4 looks closely at how an effective district shifts its policies, practices, and procedures—in particular those related to hiring and evaluation—to align with the learning mission. Chapter 5 describes how to lead the creation of collaborative teams. Chapter 6 digs into the work of those teams to focus on student learning, and chapter 7 then highlights the connections between teamwork and adult learning. Finally, chapter 8 explains the importance of evaluating progress on the journey to becoming a professional learning community. In every chapter, we share practices, examples, and tools, highlight important lessons learned, and provide reflection questions for district and school teams as well as individual readers to consider.

Reculturing schools to become professional learning communities is hard work. The issue is not simply a question of *knowing* but of *doing*, and beyond that, of *leading*—of will. There is little doubt that professional learning community concepts and practices can be a powerful force for improving school districts and thus the learning levels of students. But becoming a professional learning community requires action, courage, risk taking, and persistence. We will never change the traditional culture of school districts by seeking safe, calm harbors. We must set sail into a sea of uncertainty, knowing full well that storms and rough seas lie ahead. But we must set sail, simply because the stakes are so high. These are *our* children, our future. They deserve to be educated at high levels, not merely required to attend school.

So, for those who are committed to leaving safe harbors and calm seas and setting sail to reculturing schools into high-performing professional learning communities, it is our sincere hope that the following ideas, suggestions, and resources will assist you on your journey to become a high-performing professional learning community, because the journey is inherently worthwhile. Our desire is that each reader, after reading this book, will be motivated to declare, "We can do this!" and ask, "Why not *us*? Why not *now*?"

Chapter 1

A New Way to Lead Schools

Discussions about leadership can be much like discussions about religion: almost everyone speaks about both topics with a high degree of certainty in his or her views. Agreement about specific points and their implications for behavior is frequently lacking, however. So rather than advocate for a specific definition of leadership, we believe it is much more beneficial to describe the behaviors we have observed in leaders of professional learning communities and then to explore the effects that those leadership behaviors have on organizational development—for better or for worse. As we reflect on these behaviors, and more specifically, on the underlying, sometimes hidden assumptions that guide those behaviors, we become more conscious of the foundations of our daily work.

What we know above all is that the traditional ways of leading schools are inadequate when it comes to reculturing districts and schools into high-performing professional learning communities. The old ways of leading schools are simply not good enough anymore. Think about it: gone are the days when we assumed that just because a principal has completed a program in school administration, he or she has become magically ready to create and lead a high-performing school. And yet, although we know leadership requires more complex skills and training, year after year district leaders continue to hire principals and send them out into schools with little direction or support, as if to say, "Shoo, shoo—go lead!"

> *What we know above all is that the traditional ways of leading schools are inadequate when it comes to reculturing districts and schools into high-performing professional learning communities.*

As we share our views regarding a new way to lead, we recognize that behaviors are, to a great extent, a result of the assumptions we hold. The leadership practices described in this book are based on the following basic assumptions we hold about leaders and leadership behaviors that can have a huge impact on the reculturing of districts and schools into high-performing professional learning communities.

PLC Is *the* Initiative to Ensure Student Learning

Our primary assumption is that the professional learning community model offers our best hope for ensuring high levels of learning for all students. This belief drives what effective leaders of professional learning communities do, how they think, and how they feel.

Acting on this belief requires that leaders go far beyond simply endorsing the PLC concept; they must gain a deep, rich understanding of what professional learning communities are, how they differ from traditional schools, and how they work. They must proactively *lead* the work of reculturing their district or school into a high-performing professional learning community, and they must lead with passion and persistence!

> *Our primary assumption is that the professional learning community model offers our best hope for ensuring high levels of learning for all students.*

This energy and passion are necessary to convince educators that the PLC model will work. Traditional school culture reflects a focus on things that are beyond the control of faculty, staff, and students: prior knowledge, school funding, and so on. This focus on what we can't change leads to frustration and the shifting of responsibility, but does nothing to improve student learning.

However, some aspects of district and school culture *can* be changed—and have been shown to have a strong correlation with improved student learning. Leaders in professional learning communities ensure that the conversations, decisions, and the work reflect a focus on aspects of school culture that can be changed and that will make an impact (see fig. 1.1).

Many leaders base their leadership behavior on the assumption that the most effective way to improve schools is by implementing hot new initiatives. In district after district, school after school, they can be observed frantically implementing whatever is new, whatever the district next door is doing, one initiative after the other. The goal is to do, do, and do more. Rarely do they stick with anything long enough to see if it's getting results. Often the only results they're paying attention to are the results of the state or provincial summative assessment. Eventually, these schools (and their districts) begin to resemble a Christmas tree—covered with program ornaments of every new educational practice or fad, leaving faculty and staff feeling completely overwhelmed.

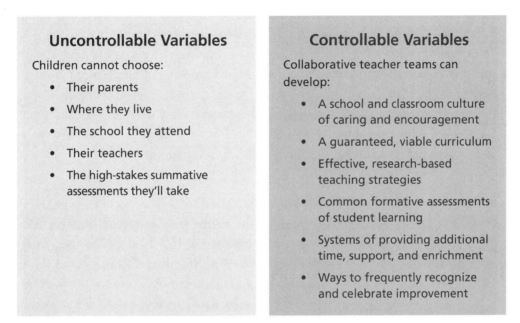

Uncontrollable Variables	Controllable Variables
Children cannot choose: • Their parents • Where they live • The school they attend • Their teachers • The high-stakes summative assessments they'll take	Collaborative teacher teams can develop: • A school and classroom culture of caring and encouragement • A guaranteed, viable curriculum • Effective, research-based teaching strategies • Common formative assessments of student learning • Systems of providing additional time, support, and enrichment • Ways to frequently recognize and celebrate improvement

Figure 1.1: Impacting student learning in a professional learning community.

In fact, these fad-driven leaders rarely equate a successful school with high levels of learning. Instead, they view success through the lens of a nice working environment in which everyone is busy—in which everyone is tired by winter break and completely worn out by June. District leaders then act surprised when learning results are disappointing.

Successful leaders view the professional learning community concept not just as another initiative or a laundry list of initiatives to improve learning. For them, becoming a professional learning community is *the* initiative. They believe that a focus on learning brings all the research related to best practice together and connects it to the day-to-day work in schools. They know that once teams begin to do PLC work, the research comes alive.

For example, when schools work on their essential outcomes (power standards), they find they're working toward Marzano's (2003) concept of a *guaranteed* curriculum. When teams talk about pacing or "chunking out" content through the school year, they're really working to ensure the curriculum is viable. They study best practices related to instruction and formative assessments, and then they learn how to provide students with additional time, support, and enrichment in each specific content area or skill where it's needed. In other words, the professional learning community concept simply serves as an umbrella over all best practices.

When a new initiative or direction is introduced in a district, many faculty and staff have the attitude of "this too shall pass." After all, that's their experience. Successful leaders send the clear and consistent message that the mission is not going to change, that we *will continue* to ensure high levels of learning for all students by embedding professional learning community concepts and practices deep into the district culture. Every school, every team, every classroom—and through them, every child—will eventually *get there*. They may not necessarily get there at the same time, but they will get there! Successful PLC leaders have truly embraced what it means to sign their contract as a school leader.

Leaders Matter

> *Successful implementation of the professional learning community concept requires* highly skilled *and effective leaders.*

The assumption that leaders matter may seem obvious. However, we are constantly amazed to find district leaders who hope that PLC *practices* will be strong enough to compensate for a few weak leaders at the building level. This just will not work! In some cases, it's as simple as this: the wrong people are in key positions, and everyone knows it. The fact is, rather than being powerful enough to compensate for weak leaders, successful implementation of the professional learning community concept *requires* highly skilled and effective leaders.

A new way to lead schools requires a new way of thinking. Those in leadership positions need to think about their thinking, simply because how and what leaders *think* drives *how others act*. However, getting people to think about their thinking is not easy. Many are content with their opinions. The most effective leaders self-reflect on their thinking and their behavior and are open to new ideas and new ways.

For example, what do we think about the fundamental purpose of schools? Is it to ensure that all students are taught the correct content in an effective and efficient manner to get all standards covered before the state assessment? Or is the core purpose of schools to ensure that all students learn, and learn at high levels? Who is responsible for setting the conditions to make this happen? Do we think schools can be more effective when teachers are left alone to teach their students, or do we think students will learn more if teachers work in collaborative teams with their colleagues? Do we think students would benefit from additional time and support when they experience difficulty with their learning, or do we think students should suffer the consequences of their choosing not to learn? What will we make time for, and how will we structure and spend our time? How we answer these, and dozens of similar questions, determines how we structure schools and how we lead them on a daily basis.

District Leadership Matters

The quality of leadership within schools is greatly affected by the quality of district office leadership, just as the quality of teacher leadership is affected by the quality of principal leadership. Although this sounds like common sense, research validates the important role district-level leadership plays in school improvement (Waters & Marzano, 2006).

Before we can expect kids to get it, or faculty and staff to get it, or parents to get it, leaders must get it. There is an old cliché in psychology that states you must be at least as healthy as the person you're trying to help. This is certainly true of clarifying the work of professional learning communities. Someone—preferably everyone—at the district office must get it. District leaders must have a deep, rich understanding of professional learning community practices and concepts, as well as the leadership and organizational skills to promote, protect, and ensure that the work gets done. Obviously, leaders must attend to numerous daily challenges, but *not* at the expense of the practices that are specifically targeted to improve student learning!

Although the quality of district leadership affects virtually every aspect of district culture, perhaps the greatest influence is on building principals. What principals do and how well they do it is greatly impacted by the expectations, modeling, and monitoring—in addition to resource allocation—of district leaders. We've come to realize there are some building leaders who don't get it, don't want to do it, and don't feel comfortable requiring others to do it. District leaders have to take "Oh well, then you don't have to do this" off the table and replace it with "How can I help you do this?"

Districts that successfully reculture themselves into professional learning communities simply begin doing the work, clarifying what a professional learning community does, and at the same time implementing professional learning community practices. They quickly engage faculty and staff in new experiences that are tied directly to student learning. In short, the most successful districts are classic examples of learning by doing.

Principals Matter—A Lot!

Teachers who attend Professional Learning Community at Work Institutes often remark, "Our principals just don't get it!" The sad fact is, it is virtually impossible to create a sustainable professional learning community with a weak or ineffective principal who doesn't get it. Principals are the only people in the position to bring all the disparate elements of effective schooling together, support and maintain them, and drill them deep into the day-to-day life of their schools.

The sad fact is, it is virtually impossible to create a sustainable professional learning community with a weak or ineffective principal who doesn't get it.

Effective principals move far beyond simply relaying district office directions to the faculty and staff. They demonstrate to all that learning is the top priority, not a matter of "if I get to it." Modeling a learning focus requires that principals own the work and take responsibility for ensuring that each collaborative team is doing the right work and doing it with high quality. This means going beyond the *must dos* and taking care of the *should dos* as well. For example, figure 1.2 illustrates what principals should do to make required classroom observations more effective: that is, to connect the focus of their observations to the work and improvement goals of the specific team of which the teacher is a member.

Figure 1.2 is based on the assumption that ensuring learning is at the very heart of the principalship. Principals need to see how all the daily tasks that are required to meet this huge responsibility align. In other words, how can the *must dos* that are associated with being a principal be logically connected to the *should dos* of being a principal in a professional learning community?

Some principals see the work associated with improving student learning as just a series of additional tasks on their to-do list. Others don't see how many of the things they already do align with PLC practices and that they really do have time to engage in their work in a meaningful way.

Effective principals connect all of their work to student learning; they use student learning data to inform everything from the school improvement plan to classroom observations and evaluation of teachers. They begin by walking teams through the process of reviewing school student achievement data to create a data portrait of their team and school. They use these data and the related discussions to lead the development of a school improvement plan that includes collaboratively developed SMART goals and highlights the things the teams will do to improve student learning in the various content areas. They use what they learn from these team meetings to inform their classroom observations and evaluations.

For example, if part of the school improvement plan focuses on narrative writing, the principal might hear team conversation on developing common narrative prompts, crafting daily learning targets that are directly related to the state standards for narrative writing, or using certain shared instructional strategies, ideas, and resources. Perhaps the discussion focuses on the use of a specific graphic organizer or specific strategies to help students elaborate in their writing, or examines the learning levels of specific students. Here's the key! Attending these team meetings *prior* to the observation allows the principal to specifically select lessons to observe that are directly tied to the school improvement plan. The preconference the principal has with the teacher can then be linked to the work that was observed in the team meeting and the learning needs of the students.

Principal *Must Dos* to Ensure High Levels of Learning

- Analyze all available student learning data.

- Develop a school improvement plan.

- Monitor team effectiveness and the guaranteed and viable curriculum by attending team meetings, reviewing the quality of team products, and monitoring team common formative assessment results.

- Monitor the effectiveness of plans for additional time, support, and enrichment.

- Complete the teacher observation and evaluation cycle.

Principal *Should Dos* to Align Observations With the Learning Focus

Preobservation	Observation	Postobservation

• Select for observation those content areas targeted by the school improvement plan.
 	
• Hold principal and teacher conversations tied to the essential standard and learning target for the lesson to be observed.
 	
• Hold principal and teacher conversations tied to the focus of team discussions and agreed-on strategies and practices for:
 	
  * Instruction
 	
  * Assessment
 	
  * Additional time, support, and enrichment
	• Look for evidence the lesson is tied to the standard and learning target.
	
	• Look for evidence of team discussion and team learning improvement goals.
	
	• Listen to student voice; do the students know what they are learning and why?
	
	• Examine what student work is being generated.
	
	• Ask, "Are the kids learning, and how do we know?"
		• Examine student work.
		
		• Ask, "Are kids learning, and how do we know?"
		
		• Ask, "What are we doing about kids who aren't learning?"
		
		• Ask, "What are we doing to extend and enrich student learning?"
		
		• Ask, "What can I do to help you?"

Figure 1.2: Aligning principal role with a focus on learning.

This specificity allows the classroom observation to take on added relevance. The principal will not be randomly observing classes simply to fulfill a state or district requirement. Instead, during the observation, the principal should see evidence of what was being discussed in the team meeting. For example, does the principal see a learning target posted? Can students tell the principal what they are learning and why it's important? Is the graphic organizer that was agreed on by the team being used? What student work is being generated as part of the lesson? The principal should be asking, "Are the students learning, and how do we know?" This is a major shift from the traditional approach to observing teachers teach.

Of course, the postconference should focus on *evidence* of student learning: student work. The conversation should focus on such questions as, Which specific students met the learning target for the lesson? Which students are struggling? What can be done to help them—what are the most appropriate interventions? How can we extend and enrich the learning of students who are meeting the learning targets? Finally, the principal should always ask, "How can I help you? Is there anything you need from me?"

> *In effective districts, principals work together to anticipate issues and questions, practice and rehearse the work that is expected of teacher teams, and share learning data and improvement ideas with their colleagues.*

Beyond supporting teacher teams, principals themselves must be contributing members of a collaborative team, such as a districtwide principal team (see chapter 5). Teachers are not the only educators who more often than not work in isolation. Many, if not most districts, reflect a culture of principal isolation as well.

In effective districts, principals work together to anticipate issues and questions, practice and rehearse the work that is expected of teacher teams, and share learning data and improvement ideas with their colleagues. In short, district leaders must create a culture in which principals move beyond thinking they are responsible for only the students in *their* school, and accept responsibility for the learning of *all students* within the district.

The measure of a successful PLC leader is simply this: are more kids continually learning more? The most effective principals weren't motivated to sign a contract because of the salary or by a desire for power. These individuals take to heart the assumption that ensuring learning for all kids is *their primary job*—not the job of an instructional coach, or the assistant principal, or a consultant. All of these people assist in important ways, but ultimately, student learning is the responsibility of the building principal.

Collaborative, Highly Dispersed Leadership Matters

There are many leaders who can successfully lead the difficult, incremental work of ensuring that students are learning at high levels. However, very few, if any, can do it alone. Schooling has become so complex that it is unreasonable to believe that a single individual, no matter how capable, can effectively lead the work alone. A new way to lead schools requires leaders who are highly skilled at creating a meaningful and effective collaborative culture in which the complex work of ensuring high levels of learning is accomplished by high-performing collaborative teams that are committed to and passionate about focusing on the right things, at the right time, and with high quality. Effective leaders of professional learning communities not only harness the power of collaborative teams, they disperse the leadership responsibility throughout the district and its schools. Everyone has leadership responsibilities and a role to play in the learning improvement process.

Here's an example of leaders utilizing the power of collaborative teaming. We often urge principals to create a "stop doing" list. But rather than simply admonishing principals to "take something off your plate," we think district leaders should guide principals to establish a school leadership team that helps with the most important work on their plate—ensuring learning for all. Determining how to make that happen involves everything from effective hiring, to designing the master schedule, to setting the structure and practices that give kids additional time and support, and, most important, to embedding layered leadership throughout the school. We'll explore more about teams in chapters 5 and 6.

Simultaneous Top-Down, Bottom-Up Leadership

There is an assumption in more traditional districts and schools that only bottom-up initiatives will be successful or should even be undertaken. But the complex journey of district reculturing is not likely to simply bubble up from the bottom. And while bottom-up leadership is desirable, by itself it is rarely enough. In every district with which we work, we emphasize the need to provide high-quality, top-down leadership, direction, and support, especially in the beginning of the PLC journey.

> *The complex journey of district reculturing is not likely to simply bubble up from the bottom. And while bottom-up leadership is desirable, by itself it is rarely enough.*

In fact, we believe that a new way to lead schools should be based on the assumption that school improvement initiatives must be *simultaneously* top down and bottom up. As depicted in figure 1.3 (page 16, moving from left to right), initial efforts to reculture districts usually are highly directive and top down.

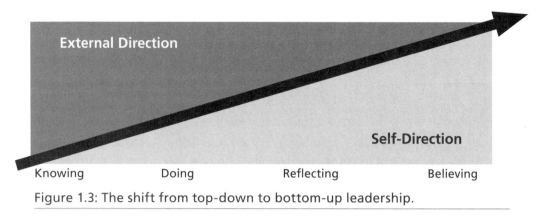

Figure 1.3: The shift from top-down to bottom-up leadership.

However, as schools and teams become engaged in the work of a learning community, and experience incremental success, they begin to gain ownership. Over time, after reaping the benefits of working in high-performing teams, educators become more knowledgeable, empowered, and experienced in acting as leaders themselves.

For these reasons, district leadership must not wait to start the PLC journey until the "time is right," "everyone is on board," or everyone fully understands everything about professional learning communities. Focusing on student learning and engaging in the work associated with becoming a professional learning community should not be optional. The right time to begin is *right now.*

Let's face it; top-down leadership has gotten a bum rap. Virtually anything that comes from the district office is suspect in many schools. It is often overlooked that almost everyone who works at the district office was once a teacher and an assistant principal or principal. One principal who moved to the district office remarked to us that he was prepared to be viewed, simply because of the move to the district, as out of touch at best and stupid at worst by faculty and staff. We concur with DuFour, DuFour, Eaker, and Many (2010), who observe, "One of the great ironies in education is that it takes strong and effective educational leaders to create truly empowered people who are capable of sustaining improvement after the leader has gone" (p. 254). In short, our assumption is that truly effective bottom-up ownership is dependent on highly effective top-down leadership.

Compassionate Leadership

Leading the work of becoming a professional learning community requires leadership that is not only both top down and bottom up but also simultaneously tight and loose, hard and soft. We believe that leaders have the ethical responsibility to be *hard* on those issues that are shown to affect student learning. At the same time, leaders must be *soft* on the people; they must respect and promote ownership and experimentation, as well as the empowerment of faculty and staff.

Effective district and school leaders recognize that *people*, not *programs*, are the heart and soul of a district or school that functions as a professional learning community. Leaders apply pressure, but for the right reasons, at the right times, and always in a respectful way. Effective district leadership behavior is described in the White River School District as "relentless pressure—gracefully applied." By this we mean that district leaders must be flexible in their implementation of professional

> *Leaders have the ethical responsibility to be* hard *on those issues that are shown to affect student learning. At the same time, leaders must be* soft *on the people; they must respect and promote ownership and experimentation, as well as the empowerment of faculty and staff.*

learning community practices and sensitive to the concerns that are raised. However, they must not equivocate in their commitment to implement professional learning community practices in order to promote high levels of learning for all students.

Will everyone be happy working under pressure, even when it is gracefully applied? Obviously not. But we take it as a compliment when people complain about the fact that their leader has a passionate and intense focus on the learning of each student.

Professional Teaching Matters

Shifting from a focus on teaching to a focus on learning is the first big idea of schools and districts that function as a professional learning community. This cultural shift is often misunderstood. A shift in focus from teaching to learning does not mean that teachers and excellent teaching

> *Not only are excellent teachers important, it is virtually impossible to have a significant impact on student learning without excellence in teaching.*

do not matter. They matter a lot! They are tremendously important. Teachers, both individually and collectively, drive the work of a professional learning community—day in and day out. Not only are excellent teachers important, it is virtually impossible to have a significant impact on student learning without excellence in teaching.

So, why the confusion? Think of it this way. In many schools, excellent teaching is viewed as the "end"—the goal. Sometimes we hear, "Our goal is to ensure excellent teaching of the state standards in every classroom." In fact, teaching is a *means* to the *end*—ensuring high levels of learning for each and every student! Our goal is not excellent teaching. Our goal is to improve student learning. Excellent teaching is but one, *although critically important*, means to this end.

It only follows, then, that one way to improve student learning is improve the quality of teaching within each classroom and team. This is where another basic tenet of a professional learning community—collective inquiry—fits. In its most simple form, collective inquiry occurs when collaborative teams seek out and utilize best practices in their classrooms, and best practices are essential for one purpose: improved student learning.

Collaborative Teacher Teams

What would it be like to teach in a professional learning community? Perhaps the most striking difference would be this: rather than teaching in a culture of teacher isolation, all teachers in the school would be expected to be contributing members of collaborative teams.

What collaborative team members *do* in a professional learning community goes far beyond casual collaborative conversations. A PLC gives great care to the makeup of each team, with the primary organizing idea being that team members should teach, generally, the same content. How teams are organized varies by school level and size (see DuFour et al., 2008, for more on possible team structures). However the teams are organized, the point is, in a professional learning community, teachers have a *shared purpose* for serving on a particular collaborative team, and that purpose is to improve student learning. To that end, the work of collaborative teacher teams focuses on the four critical questions of learning that drive the work of a professional learning community.

> *Collaborative teams of teachers, doing the right work, can achieve what individual teachers cannot achieve by working alone.*

And the simple fact is this: *teams of teachers* can more effectively do the work associated with the critical questions of learning than *individual teachers* working in isolation. Collaborative teams of teachers, doing the right work, can achieve what individual teachers cannot achieve by working alone. Following are examples of how effective collaborative teams focus on the critical questions of learning.

What Do We Want Students to Learn?

After developing critical foundational pieces such as team norms to guide its future interactions, the team begins its work with an intense study of the state (or provincial) and national curriculum standards.

While teachers who teach in more traditional schools are certainly familiar with standards, especially the ones that have been developed by their state department of education or provincial ministry, it is generally left to individual teachers to interpret the meaning and the relative importance of each standard. In schools that function as professional learning communities, collaborative teams of teachers literally become students of the standards, clarifying the meaning of each standard and developing common pacing guides to ensure adequate time is being given to the *essential* learning outcomes—or as Doug Reeves (2002) refers to them, the *power standards*.

Collaborative teacher teams then develop a guaranteed and viable curriculum (Marzano, 2003). Simply put, students are *guaranteed* the same mathematics curriculum, for example, regardless of the teachers they are assigned or the school they attend. Additionally, because teacher teams collaborate about the amount of time needed to effectively teach each standard, the curriculum is also *viable*.

Once teams, and ultimately the entire district, have developed a guaranteed and viable curriculum, the teams drill deeper into their work. They focus their discussions on questions such as, What would student work look like if this particular standard was met? In more traditional schools, even when teachers align their instruction to the standards, there can be a wide disparity between teachers' expectations for high-quality student performance. Collaboratively developing rubrics for high-quality student work naturally leads to discussions about common scoring of student products and reporting of pupil progress.

Teaching in a professional learning community means that teachers—and students—benefit from collaborative planning. In addition to clarifying and adding meaning to state and national standards, team members engage in rich discussions around unit planning. They not only collaboratively review the standards the unit should cover, they also discuss preassessment ideas and share instructional strategies and materials, develop quick checks for understanding, and share ideas about how to provide students with appropriate practice and high-quality feedback.

How Will We Know if Students Are Learning?

Clarifying and adding meaning to curricular standards is the foundational work of a collaborative team. Once that work is complete, the team next moves to the rather logical question, How will we know if our students are learning? Collaborative teams in professional learning communities develop common formative assessments in order to monitor the learning of each student, *skill by skill*, on a frequent and timely basis.

Collaborative teams in professional learning communities pursue a cultural shift from an almost exclusive reliance on summative assessments to a balanced assessment approach that relies heavily on more frequent, collaboratively developed, common formative assessments. Being a teacher in a professional learning community means being part of a collaborative team that recognizes students are more apt to perform well on high-stakes summative assessments if the quality of their learning is regularly monitored along the way—especially when the results of the assessments are used to provide students with additional time, support, or enrichment.

A visitor sitting in on team collaboration in a PLC would observe teachers collaboratively planning units of instruction and analyzing student learning data and products. The teachers would set goals, share instructional strategies, discuss assessment results item by item, highlight strengths in student learning, identify areas of concern, select interventions, evaluate the effectiveness of their assessments, learn from each other's strengths, and monitor the learning of each student, skill by skill. In short, they would drill deep into the learning of their students and their effectiveness as a team.

What Will We Do When Students Don't Learn or Need Enrichment?

The power of formative assessments lies in how they are utilized. Since students learn at different rates and in different ways, a professional learning community recognizes that some students will struggle with their learning. When they do, they need additional time and support—within the school day.

In traditional schools, teachers are left to fend for themselves when they realize some kids just aren't getting it. The fact is, there is only so much the most well-intentioned and talented teachers can do by themselves simply because the number of students who need additional time and support is often too great, and the range of needs too wide. In traditional schools, the absence of a schoolwide, systematic plan to provide struggling students with additional time and support sets up both students and teachers for failure. On the other hand, teachers in schools that function as professional learning communities have the benefit of a systematic, *schoolwide plan* of tiered interventions that provides help when students experience difficulty in their learning. If a school does everything else, even at a high level of quality, but fails to provide additional time and support when students experience difficulty in their learning, the school's effectiveness will be problematic.

Further, schools that function as professional learning communities recognize it is their *moral* obligation to help these struggling students. As DuFour, DuFour,

Eaker, and Many (2010) observe, "It is disingenuous for any school to claim its purpose is to help all students learn at high levels and then fail to create a system of intervention to give struggling learners additional time and support for learning" (p. 104). At its most basic level, providing additional time and support to students who are experiencing difficulty is simply providing *all* students with the help each of us would want for our own child.

What does additional time and support look like in a school that functions as a professional learning community? Following the advice of DuFour, DuFour, Eaker, and Many (2010), first and foremost, it is a *systematic plan* that is *timely* and *directive*, rather than merely invitational. Because the plan is composed of a series of sequential tiers, students benefit from ever-increasing focused support based on their level of need. Initially, most interventions occur within the classroom. For example, a teacher simply might reteach a particular skill set. Perhaps students who demonstrated proficiency might assist students who are struggling. However, some students may need the benefit of more intense interventions such as a tutor, or time in a mathematics lab, or a specific math program. In a professional learning community, students have the benefit of planned interventions designed to help them learn each essential skill.

Of course, not all students need additional time and support. Many students demonstrate proficiency in their learning, and yet, they could learn more. All schools have students who make excellent grades, but are under-learning. In most schools it is left up to individual teachers to develop ways to enrich or extend student learning. Again, there is only so much even the most dedicated teachers can do by themselves. Being a teacher in a professional learning community means having the benefit of a schoolwide plan to enrich and extend student learning far beyond proficiency.

> *At its most basic level, providing additional time and support to students who are experiencing difficulty is simply providing* all *students with the help each of us would want for our own child.*

A Constant Pursuit of Learning

Teaching in a school that functions as a professional learning community requires deep discussions about topics that are rarely addressed in traditional schools, yet have a huge impact on student learning. For example, teams study the best that is known about effective grading and homework policies and practices. They build shared knowledge by referring to resources such as John Hattie's (2009) review and synthesis of literally hundreds of research studies. They collaboratively address such questions as, What is the purpose of homework? How much homework is appropriate? How much weight will homework count in grading? What happens when students do not complete their homework or if it is completed incorrectly? In traditional schools, these questions—and many more like them—are left almost entirely to the discretion of individual teachers. Teaching in a professional learning community means that *teacher teams* tackle important and complex issues that have a huge impact on student learning.

A Matter of Will and Passion

For districts that wish to become professional learning communities, the scope of the work ahead is clearly broad and deep. Sadly, we have observed many districts and schools that refer to themselves as professional learning communities, yet show little evidence that professional learning community practices are deeply embedded in the district or school culture. And unless professional learning community practices are embedded at the deepest level of the classroom, to impact teachers and teaching, they will have very little, if any, impact on student learning.

To truly reculture districts and schools, leaders have to drill down into the work of a professional learning community at the faculty, staff, and student level. These leaders must possess not only the requisite knowledge and skills but also the will and the passion to delve into issues that traditionally have been largely unexamined in North America's schools. Most educators know the kind of schools, classrooms, and even lessons they would want for their own child. We desperately need leaders who are driven to reach that standard of excellence for all children. We need leaders who aren't afraid to make bold commitments like those the leaders in White River made when they declared, "The kids most in need will receive the most help from the most skilled staff." We need leaders who follow through and work out the bugs in a master schedule that provides additional time and support for kids who are struggling with their learning. We need leaders who persistently tweak that schedule, because it won't be perfect on the first attempt. We desperately need leaders who are willing to push against negative adult behavior and adult deficit thinking—who will say, "This district has proclaimed a mission of ensuring high levels of learning for all kids, and whether or not we will do the necessary work is no longer a choice."

Effective leaders know that, ultimately, leadership must touch the emotions. They know their commitment must ignite a shared commitment throughout the school or district.

But even the will to do all this is not enough. Many leaders do the right things, they're even engaged in the right work, but they suffer from a *passion gap*. Their energy and enthusiasm are invisible to others. Effective leaders know that, ultimately, leadership must touch the emotions. They know their commitment must ignite a shared commitment throughout the school or district. These leaders envision dreams and instill hope. They motivate and inspire. They constantly ask themselves, "Is my passion for improving the learning of our kids visible? Is it creating a contagious sense of excitement?"

Reflections

It is our hope that by sharing our assumptions about the leadership behaviors required for successful reculturing of districts and schools into high-performing professional learning communities, others will reflect on and discuss their own assumptions. This reflection and dialogue are foundational for reculturing any organization, since our assumptions undergird and drive our behaviors, and in turn the effects of our behaviors shape our attitudes and impact our beliefs, as well as those of others. We suggest district leaders use our assumptions as a starting point for reflection on their personal assumptions, as well as a springboard for meaningful discussions with various groups within the school or district.

Individually or in teams, reflect on questions such as the following.

1. If a visitor spent a week watching administrators, faculty, and staff going about their day-to-day work in your district or school, what patterns of behavior would he or she observe?

2. What are the underlying assumptions that drive the behavior that visitors would see in your district or school?

3. To what degree is your behavior congruent with the beliefs you profess? For example, if your stated belief is that the fundamental purpose of schools is to ensure all students learn, how is that statement reflected in behavior?

4. Have you either led or been a part of deep, rich discussions about the underlying assumptions that drive behavior within your district or school? How might such discussions be beneficial? What would be a meaningful way to conduct such discussions?

5. What are the most essential leadership behaviors required of principals in schools seeking to function as PLCs and significantly impact student learning? What mechanisms are in place, or should be in place, in your district to assist principals in acquiring or improving these skills?

6. In your district, are principals organized into collaborative teams? What do principals do at these principal team meetings? How could their collaborative teaming be enhanced? How is the effectiveness of

teacher teams directly impacted by the effectiveness of the principal team or teams?

7. How does your district or school assist teachers in acquiring best practices?

8. Is your school organized in collaborative teams? How clear is the principal on what teams should be doing? Does every team in your school focus on the critical questions of learning? How could the effectiveness of collaborative teams be enhanced in your district or school?

Chapter 2

Articulating a Moral Purpose

The challenge facing leaders who seek to reculture their districts into high-performing professional learning communities is not convincing faculty and staff that ensuring high levels of learning is an admirable and worthwhile mission. The idea that a district should seek to ensure high levels of learning for all students is hardly controversial, and it is highly unlikely that a group of faculty or staff will start a petition in opposition to learning! In fact, the inherent danger is that our mission is so common sense, it risks becoming a cliché. Rather, the challenge is *how to articulate this moral purpose in such a way that it will cause everyone to question and align his or her existing attitudes, commitments, and behaviors.* In other words, the challenge is how to embed the learning mission into the day-to-day culture throughout the district.

Most faculty and staff are willing to work hard and go above and beyond what typically might be expected—*if* they believe the purpose is worthwhile. This is why it is critical that district leaders go to extraordinary lengths to articulate the district's fundamental mission and moral purpose.

> *Most faculty and staff are willing to work hard and go above and beyond what typically might be expected—if they believe the purpose is worthwhile.*

Leaders must continually draw everyone's attention to the *why* question—why we are doing what we're doing—and this *why* must always put students and their learning, the very reason schools exist, at the center of our work.

We urge district leaders to think of their mission of ensuring high levels of learning for all students as fulfilling a sacred promise. Each morning parents literally hand over their children to us! In our experience, parents expect three things in return: (1) they want their children to be safe and secure while in our care, (2) they want them to feel special, and (3) they want them to learn—not simply to be taught, but to learn! We have the highest obligation to fulfill this promise, and everything we do in schools—every decision, every policy, every practice—should reflect this. What we do sends a much more significant message than what we say. A district that sets out on a journey to ensure high levels of learning for all students must examine everything, screen every practice, by asking, "Is this consistent with our core purpose of ensuring high levels of learning for all students?"

Perhaps the single most important thing about articulating a moral purpose is that we cannot wait until everyone is convinced. We must believe, deep in our souls, that focusing intensely and passionately on ensuring high levels of learning for all students is the *right* thing to do. Since there is virtually unanimous agreement among researchers and practitioners regarding the power of professional learning community practices to improve student learning (see DuFour et al., 2008), we believe it's simply unethical to ignore such a compelling body of evidence. It is the district leaders' job to implement the best available concepts and practices in order to positively impact student learning, and to that end, leaders cannot allow individual naysayers to opt out of the work or hold an entire district hostage, keeping faculty and staff from doing the right things for the right reasons. Even those who aren't particularly motivated by the moral purpose of ensuring student learning would have to agree that at a very minimum they are being paid to implement best practices in their school or classroom in order to improve student learning. Effective leaders work to appeal to educators' intrinsic motivation to serve students, however, knowing that the journey to become a professional learning community will require more commitment than a mere paycheck can buy.

Start With the School Board

Since the legal authority and responsibility for local public education rest with school boards, begin by ensuring your board understands the fundamental concepts and practices of professional learning communities and, more importantly, *why* it is important to implement PLC practices: to ensure that all students learn at high levels. Make clear that the work of the district must focus on achieving this result not just in one school, or a few schools, but in *all* schools. School board members receive a barrage of questions from the community, and they need to be informed so that they can help explain what's happening. As you form your guiding coalition, make working with the school board a top priority.

For many districts, like White River, this requires first educating the school board about actual student learning levels within the district, including areas in which students are performing well and areas in which students are struggling. This means taking a hard look at all aspects of student learning data—not just at one meeting, but at many meetings, as data become an ongoing focus of discussion and interaction. We urge district leaders to present data in comparisons whenever possible. For example, how do your students compare with state and national norms? How do they compare with other districts in the area? How do current data compare with previous years? Is the district improving?

Refocus the District Mission, Vision, Values, and Goals

These data discussions will usually spark the need to collaboratively revisit and refocus the district's mission and other foundational documents. Now, no district or school has ever made significant improvement merely by rewriting its mission statement. On the other hand, rich collaborative discussions about the district's fundamental purpose can build a valuable framework for future work. In fact, we believe it is simply impossible to achieve a district's fundamental purpose of ensuring high levels of learning for all students unless we are absolutely clear about:

- The core of the enterprise (our mission)
- The kind of school district we would like to become (our vision)
- The attitudes, behaviors, and commitments we will need to promote, protect, and defend if we are going to fulfill our mission (our values)
- The steps we need to take and when we will take them (our goals)

For a more detailed exploration of this topic, see chapters 5 and 6 in *Revisiting Professional Learning Communities at Work* (DuFour et al., 2008).

One reason building this foundation is so difficult is that many faculty and staff view writing mission and vision statements as a waste of time that has little to do with the day-to-day work of classrooms and schools. Since our attitudes are usually the result of our experiences, it is little wonder faculty and staff take a dim view of any activity or initiative associated with writing mission or vision statements. However, once faculty and staff see how the district mission, vision, values, and goals are being utilized throughout the district, they become vitally interested in their development.

How well this work gets done depends on the quality of leadership guiding the process. Of course, leadership at the central office level is critical, but the leadership ability of each principal will determine how well the foundation is developed and embedded in each school. But the leadership capability of principals isn't nearly enough. At each step along the way, those who are charged with developing a shared sense of mission, vision, values, and goals must be given the training, resources, and most important, examples to assist them in doing their work at a high level of quality.

In most districts, this refocusing involves two distinct phases. The first is to clearly articulate the district mission and other foundational documents. In White River, for example, we emphasized that the district mission should be straightforward, disarmingly direct, clear, and brief: "The mission of the White River School District is to ensure high levels of learning for all students to prepare them for success beyond high school." The second, more challenging phase, and the topic of the remainder of this book, is to continually and consistently embed professional learning community concepts and practices in virtually every aspect of culture in order to fulfill the district's core purpose—its very reason for existing. The mission of ensuring high levels of learning for all students is simply too important to file away or gather dust on a shelf.

> *While it's important to build a deep foundation for PLC practices, we have also learned the importance of not wallowing in the work—that is, not spending a tremendous amount of time on things that should be completed fairly quickly.*

While it's important to build a deep foundation for PLC practices, we have also learned the importance of not wallowing in the work—that is, not spending a tremendous amount of time on things that should be completed fairly quickly. The key issue is not in how long it takes to develop these foundational pieces but rather how they are utilized—day in and day out. We have worked with districts that spent in excess of a full year on the process of refining the district mission and vision. It is much better to articulate the mission and vision in a meaningful, practical, commonsense way, and then move on to *doing the work* associated with reculturing the district into a professional learning community.

In White River, for example, we did not spend a long time seeking an answer to why White River School District existed. Instead, we spent time building shared knowledge and making sure everyone *understood* the answer: to ensure high levels of learning for all students. (We'll talk more about the important process of building shared knowledge in chapter 3.) And we then spent considerable time in collaborative discussions about the ramifications a learning mission has for everyone, regardless of role, and what a learning mission would look like in classrooms, schools, and school districts if we really meant it. Figure 2.1 shows the first draft of administrative cabinet commitments that resulted from early discussions at the leadership level.

The White River School District has proclaimed a mission of ensuring high levels of learning for all students for success beyond high school. In order to achieve this mission, the administrative cabinet will focus our work by adhering to the following shared commitments.

In our role as the administrative cabinet of the White River School District, we will:

- Make student learning the primary focus of our work and the work of others throughout the district and our primary framework for decision making

- Provide the encouragement, support, training, and resources necessary to enhance the capacity of those within each building to fulfill their mission of ensuring high levels of learning for all students

- Clearly understand and articulate the functions of each administrative unit within the district and respect the work of each unit by working directly and exclusively with those who have primary responsibility for the success of each unit

- Create a collaborative culture that models respect for each other, our students, faculty and staff, administrators, parents, and the larger community

- Conduct the work of the district primarily through the work of high-performing collaborative teams

- Make decisions that are primarily research-based and data driven

- Monitor our success in multiple ways, but primarily by our impact on student learning

- Create a professional atmosphere in which we model the behavior we expect of others

Figure 2.1: Sample commitments draft.

Source: White River School District. Used with permission.

We urge districts to follow the advice of DuFour and Eaker (1998) and engage virtually all faculty and staff (district and building level) in rich discussion around the issues that collectively form the foundation of a professional learning community. First examine the current reality of learning levels across the district, and then collaboratively describe the district and school you seek to become: the vision. Clarify the values that will promote, protect, defend, and celebrate the mission. Commit to specific behaviors that will drive those values into daily work throughout the district. Create goals to define, in detail, what steps you must take and when to make sure that your students are learning at high levels and you are becoming the kind of district you hope to become.

Make Goal Setting Meaningful

Clearly articulating mission, vision, and values or commitments will be of little value unless they are a catalyst for purposeful action. In many cases, administrators, faculty, and staff view goal setting as busywork—something to turn in, mark off the to-do list, and then forget.

Meaningful goal setting causes personnel across the district to *set priorities* and *act*. Meaningful goals serve another purpose as well. They create the conditions for short-term wins that can keep the momentum for district reculturing going strong. To make goal setting a useful and meaningful endeavor:

- Goals should be tied directly to student achievement.
- Goals should be connected directly to the district's core purpose, vision, and values and commitments.
- Goals should be collaboratively developed.
- Goals should be clearly communicated and widely distributed.
- Goals should be utilized for decision making.
- Progress toward attaining the goals should be frequently monitored, coupled with specific feedback.
- Appropriate resources for attaining the goals should be provided.
- A consistent format for goals should be utilized across the district to ensure consistency and quality.

We are often asked about the format or rubric for writing and evaluating goals. The SMART goal format (Conzemius & O'Neil, 2005) is used in White River and in many districts that are implementing professional learning community practices. DuFour et al. (2008) summarize the SMART goal acronym as:

- *__Strategic__ and __Specific__—The goal is linked to the organization's purpose and vision and sufficiently specific to avoid ambiguity or confusion.*

- *__Measurable__—The organization has established baseline measures from which to assess progress.*

- *__Attainable__—People in the organization believe that with collective effort they can accomplish the goal.*

- *__Results-Oriented__—The goal focuses on outcomes rather than inputs and results rather than intentions. Once again, because the purpose and priority in schools and districts* *should be higher levels of student learning, a SMART goal will call for evidence of improved student achievement, and it will be student-centered rather than project-centered or teacher-centered.*

- ***Timebound****—The goal should include a timeframe for when specific action will be taken and when it is anticipated the goal will be accomplished. (pp. 159–160)*

Connect Ideas to Actions

Since many faculty and staff hold the attitude that mission and vision statements and other foundational documents are rarely used, it is critical that district leaders demonstrate from the very beginning of the process that the results of these collaborative discussions will form the cornerstone of the district's decision making in such areas as policy development, budgeting and resource allocation, staff development activities, hiring, and personnel performance appraisal. We'll explore some examples of just how the mission is applied to decisions in chapter 4. It is absolutely essential that faculty and staff see the foundation pieces being used, rather than simply framed and displayed in the district office lobby.

Even then, however, just because your mission and vision sound great doesn't mean faculty and staff will really believe them, deep down. You have to do the work, and more than that, you must do the *right* work! Faculty and staff in the districts with which we have worked, particularly in White River, began to realize the district leadership really meant it only when the district office and schools were organized into collaborative teams, and when the work of the teams focused on student learning. They took note when district leaders aligned policies, practices, and procedures with the learning mission. They realized there really was going to be a focus on student learning when each school changed its schedule so that students could receive additional time, support, and enrichment within the school day. In short, district leaders learned that actually *doing the work* associated with improving student learning sends a much more significant message than rewriting a mission statement.

This connection between word and deed needs to be explicit. In White River, we continuously pointed out the connection between the ideas we professed and our actions, decisions, and policies. For example, we repeatedly used phrases like:

- "Because our mission is to . . ."
- "Because we said we want to be a district that . . ."
- "Because we made a commitment to . . ."
- "Because we set a goal to . . ."

Don't hope that faculty and staff will see the connection; emphasize the connection at every opportunity.

Revisit and Revise

The fundamental questions that form the foundation of a professional learning community will take on increased and new meaning as the district engages in the work. Therefore, districts should periodically revisit their foundation documents and ask if they need to be refined in order to become more useful and relevant. We have found this to be especially true of the shared values and commitments agreements.

For example, in 2006, district leaders in the White River School District collaboratively developed the foundational pieces as they began their journey to becoming a professional learning community. However, by the fall of 2010, they had a much deeper understanding of why the shared commitments piece was such a crucial and powerful tool for shaping district culture—and thus revised the commitments to reflect new understandings. Figure 2.2 shows an example of the results of such discussions.

Effective districts are constantly tweaking their practices in order to be more effective and communicating to everyone within the district that this drive for continuous improvement is expected to be shared by all, and that the pursuit of the district's core purpose will remain constant.

This consistency of message was emphasized in White River in the August back-to-school message and at the annual leadership retreat. Rather than explaining all the new things that were happening, at these pivotal moments, White River focused on what was going to remain the *same*. This consistency of focus and message helped administrators, faculty, and staff develop confidence that improving student learning by embedding professional learning community practices in every school, team, and classroom would remain the district's focus year after year.

District Climate and Culture

The White River School District is committed to developing a caring, inviting, and encouraging climate and culture for both students and adults. The district climate and culture must be conducive to learning and personal growth. The climate and culture of the White River District will:

- Monitor learning progress, behavior, and the emotional well-being of each student and provide additional time and support if needed

- Ensure a physically and emotionally safe and civil school environment for students and staff

- Treat all members of the school community with mutual respect, consideration, and support

- Reflect an atmosphere of caring and cooperation

- Emphasize meaningful, high-quality collaboration throughout the district

- Ensure open communication between all members of the school community—students, staff, parents, and community

- Make a conscious effort to recognize and celebrate the individual and collective efforts of students and staff

Leadership

In order to fulfill the mission of ensuring high levels of learning for all students, the White River School District is dependent on high-quality shared leadership. Successful leadership:

- Promotes and protects the district's mission, vision, and shared commitments

- Provides the resources and support that are necessary for staff to meet expectations

- Models the belief that all students can learn and that district educators have a large degree of influence on the degree to which students succeed

- Builds shared leadership by providing meaningful leadership opportunities for entire staff

Collaborative Culture

The White River School District is committed to creating a collaborative culture that is characterized by the utilization of high-performing collaborative teams that:

Figure 2.2: White River School District vision, 2008–2010.   Continued➜

Source: White River School District. Used with permission.

- Focus on the critical questions associated with ensuring high levels of learning for all students

- Work interdependently to achieve common learning goals for which they are held mutually accountable

- Analyze student learning data for the purpose of making instructional changes to meet learner needs and for the purpose of improving professional practice

- Take collective responsibility for learning for all kids

- Take collective responsibility for results

Curriculum and Instruction

Attainment of the White River School District's mission of ensuring high levels of learning for all students requires a balanced curriculum that stimulates intellectual curiosity, teaches students how to learn, and assists students in becoming fulfilled, productive, and effective citizens. The curriculum of the district will:

- Be aligned with the Washington State Essential Academic Learning Requirements and Grade Level Expectations

- Be collaboratively planned

- Ensure a rigorous guaranteed and viable curriculum that is aligned with district standards and is planned, taught, and, most important, learned

- Define essential knowledge, skills, and dispositions students must acquire in each grade, subject, and course

- Frequently monitor student learning utilizing a variety of approaches, including collaboratively developed common formative assessments as well as summative assessments

- Provide additional time and support for students who experience difficulty in their learning

- Provide enrichment for students who demonstrate mastery of state and district standards

- Encourage a wide variety of research-based teaching strategies and styles

- Stimulate active engagement of students in each class

- Be monitored, evaluated, and revised on a timely and regular basis

- Be selected in accordance with our adopted policies and procedures

- Provide effective instruction for students at Tier 1, Tier 2, and Tier 3

- Provide frequent opportunities for student feedback

- Reflect research-based instructional strategies

Assessment

The White River School District is committed to providing a high-quality assessment program that reflects the Washington State Essential Academic Learning Requirements and Grade Level Expectations as well as district academic standards. It will provide student assessment data at the district, school, classroom, and individual student levels. The assessment program will:

- Be implemented in alignment with the state assessment system
- Provide student outcome data at the district, building, classroom, and individual student levels
- Be developed and implemented in a manner consistent with the most current research
- Assist the district in making systemic change
- Fairly and equitably assess all students
- Be used at all levels to make decisions about what is best for students and to improve instructional practice
- Reflect use of both formative and summative assessments
- Use technology to assure the student assessment information is readily available to staff

Parent, School, and Community Relations

Parents entrust the White River School District with the safety and education of their children. The entire staff views this responsibility as a sacred trust. We believe that student success is enhanced when the district develops exemplary programs that connect schools with parents and the larger community. Such programs will:

- Promote successful parent, school, and community partnerships
- Welcome parents as partners and value their support and assistance
- Ensure effective two-way communication
- Provide timely information about student learning
- Provide multiple avenues for parents to become partners in their child's education

High-Quality Staff

The district is committed to hiring, retaining, supporting, and developing a staff that demonstrates practice congruent with the values and mission of the district. The White River staff will:

- Focus on ensuring that all students learn
- Engage in productive, positive, and meaningful collaboration in order to improve professional practice and student learning

Continued➜

- Establish a classroom environment conducive to high levels of learning for all students
- Ensure that the collection and analysis of evidence of student learning, and adjusting instruction accordingly, is an essential element of daily practice
- Utilize a variety of research-based practices in instruction, assessment, technology, cultural sensitivity, and grading and reporting
- Model continuous learning, reflection, adaptation, and professional growth
- Demonstrate professional behavior at all times

Students

Students are at the very heart of the White River School District. Ultimately, our success as a school district is based on the character, conduct, and learning levels of our students. In the White River School District, students will:

- Be encouraged and supported in the pursuit of personal and career goals
- Understand the learning targets they are expected to achieve and the criteria used to monitor the quality of their work
- Become more self-directed learners as they progress through school, accepting responsibility for their learning, decisions, and actions
- Become actively engaged in both the academic and nonacademic areas of school
- Give their best effort
- Be considerate of others—both their fellow students and adults
- Conduct themselves in a way that contributes to a safe and orderly atmosphere and respects the rights of others

Technology and Learning

The White River School District is committed to an active, student-centered learning environment. Technology, through skilled and developed use, empowers students, staff, and community to access, utilize, and communicate information globally as well as locally. The effective use of technology will assist students in becoming perceptive and discerning individuals, critical problem solvers, contributing members of society, and lifelong learners. In order to support this vision, White River school leadership and staff will:

- Work to secure funding in order to provide equitable access to technology resources for all staff and students
- Ensure that acquired technology resources are integrated across the K–12 curriculum

- Model 21st century skills in their own learning and work experiences
- Provide students with instruction on how to analyze information for content, relevancy, and accuracy, and how to apply the information in real-world situations
- Pursue best practices in learning how to use technology to differentiate instructional practices to better meet the needs of diverse learning styles

Professional Development

The White River School District prides itself in modeling professional learning community practices and concepts. Nowhere is this more evident than in the professional learning and development of its staff. In the White River District, professional development will:

- Be based on an analysis of student learning data and school and team goals
- Provide high-quality, job-embedded, systematic, focused professional development for all staff
- Embed ongoing professional development into the routine work of all staff through the professional learning communities model as well as other structures
- Demonstrate a commitment to the professional growth of all staff, with a focus on analyzing evidence of student learning and self-reflection
- Leverage the expertise, talent, and leadership in the district in order to provide high-quality, meaningful professional development
- Be monitored, evaluated, and adjusted regularly to ensure an impact on student learning

Figure 2.2: White River School District vision, 2008–2010.

Source: White River School District. Used with permission.

Ask the Right Questions

When a school district articulates learning as its fundamental purpose and strives to make the cultural shift from ensuring that all students are taught to ensuring that all students learn, everyone within the district will start to ask fundamentally different questions about his or her work. A question that is frequently asked is, "What is a professional learning community, anyway?" What makes this question difficult is that it implies that a professional learning community is a *something*—an entity. At its most basic level, however, being a professional learning community is really applying *a way of thinking* to every aspect of district culture. The professional learning community concept simply provides a framework for connecting best practices and achieving high levels of learning for students and adults.

Because faculty and staff in professional learning communities think differently, they "do" differently than their colleagues in more traditional schools. Professional learning communities are grounded in the belief that if we really mean it when we say the purpose of schools is to ensure high levels of learning for all students, we ask fundamentally different questions. And because we are asking different questions, we behave in fundamentally different ways.

Effective leaders work to ensure that the right people ask the right questions, at the right time, and in the right context. Key questions should collectively send a consistent message emphasizing student learning. In order to make sure we move beyond merely declaring our commitment to student learning, we urge district leaders to frequently—and with passion and a sense of urgency—ask, "What would ensuring high levels of learning look like *if we really meant it?*" In White River, we found this question helped us focus our work on doing the right things for the right reasons.

Of course, simply doing the right things does not address the issue of quality—how well we do what we do. In order to make sure they address the issue of quality, we urge the faculty and staff in districts with which we work to filter their assumptions, decisions, attitudes, and behaviors through the question, Would this be good enough for my own child?

> *We urge the faculty and staff in districts with which we work to filter their assumptions, decisions, attitudes, and behaviors through the question, Would this be good enough for my own child?*

Most parents know the kind of school they would like their children to attend and the kinds of lessons they would like their children to experience. In fact, most district leaders have listened to parents make a case for their child to be in a certain classroom with a certain teacher! In traditional districts, parents are engaged in a perpetual quest of trying to weave their students into the best school with the best teachers. In White River and other districts in which we have worked, we have found there is no lack of knowledge about the kind of schools, classrooms, and lessons we should provide; the issue is *guaranteeing* high-quality schools, classrooms, and lessons for *every* student. The decision to become a professional learning community is a decision to stop operating like an educational lottery and serve a higher moral purpose.

DuFour and Eaker (1998) point out that one way to determine what an organization *really* values is by answering questions such as:

- What do we spend our time *planning* for?
- On what do we allocate our *resources*?
- What *questions* are we attempting to answer?
- What behaviors are we *modeling*?
- What behaviors are we willing to *confront*?
- What do we *monitor*?
- What do we *celebrate*?

Periodically reflecting on these questions helps district leaders make sure they are communicating a clear moral purpose by their own behavior, rather than simply telling others what to do; giving orders never results in systematic change.

As districts begin to collaboratively address these questions, what faculty and staff do and how they do it begins to shift. They realize that the district cannot achieve its mission without addressing four critical questions centered on student learning (DuFour, DuFour, Eaker, & Many, 2010)—questions that clarify the work that occurs in a professional learning community—and they cannot successfully answer these questions if they continue to work in a culture of teacher (and principal) isolation.

For example, in White River, we realized that if we really meant it (and this is a critical *if!*) when we said we wanted to ensure all students learned, we obviously needed to collaboratively address the question, Learn what? And if we were clear on what we wanted students to learn, we still needed to address the question, How will we know they've learned it? Of course, we knew students learned at different rates and in different ways, so we needed to ask, "What will we do when some students experience difficulty in their learning?" and "What will we do to enrich and enhance the learning of students who demonstrate proficiency?" Addressing these questions enabled us to begin to look and act like a professional learning community.

Monitor What You Say You Value

It makes little sense to think we will convince faculty and staff of the significance of our mission to ensure high levels of learning if we then spend our time and energy monitoring other things. Faculty, staff, and students learn what we are really passionate about by what we check on. A district

"Are the students learning, and how do we know?" drives district efforts to monitor the learning of every student in every classroom—student by student, skill by skill.

that claims to be a professional learning community will constantly ask, "Are the students learning? How do we know? Show me."

In successful districts, this question is addressed in multiple ways at both the district level and in individual schools, but is most central to the work of collaborative teacher teams. And as districts work to drill this question deep into the culture of each team, they do so with great specificity—and importantly, passion. "Are the students learning, and how do we know?" drives district efforts to monitor the learning of every student in every classroom—student by student, skill by skill. We'll explore specific monitoring tools and strategies in the chapters to come.

Keep Returning to Why

Sometimes administrators, faculty, and staff confuse the means (embedding the professional learning community concept and practices) with the end (ensuring high levels of learning for all students). The mission is not to become a professional learning community but to ensure learning. We have found that district leaders must make every effort to consciously connect what the district is doing with the *why*—constantly and clearly articulating that this work is about our kids and their learning.

Let's face it, the vast majority of faculty and staff work very hard, and they get tired. Working hard and being tired is simply part of an educator's life. The key to effective leadership is to make sure faculty and staff are working hard and getting tired by doing the right things! This is the difference between working hard and being frustrated, or working hard and feeling *fulfilled* due to the fact that more kids are learning more.

We believe faculty and staff want to do the right things, and they want their students to learn. We've seen educators put forth extraordinary effort when they believe in what they are being asked to do. So, in the hectic, day-to-day work of schools, leaders must continually draw the attention of everyone back to the students and their learning.

Make it personal and urgent. Always focus the conversations around the concept of "our kids," using names of children whenever possible. In meetings and presentations, use every opportunity to embed pictures and video clips of students—and faculty—from within the district. Make every effort to move faculty and staff from thinking of student learning as a worthwhile but abstract concept to thinking of student learning as the learning of my child, my relative's child, my friend's child, my neighbor's child. Constantly relate the work to what faculty and staff would want for their own children. Ask questions such as:

- "When you send your own children to school, don't you expect the teachers to have a clear and concise understanding of what is essential for them to learn, regardless of the school they attend or the teacher to whom they are assigned?"

- "Wouldn't you expect there to be a system in place to monitor your child's learning, skill by skill?"

- "If your child experienced difficulty in learning, wouldn't you expect your child to receive meaningful additional time and support?"

- "Even though your child may demonstrate proficiency, wouldn't you expect the school to have a system in place to extend and enrich your child's learning?"

Help educators realize they not only have the responsibility, they have the *power* to change lives, forever. They can be heroes every day.

Celebrate, Celebrate, Celebrate

We celebrate what we value, and by celebrating, we *communicate* what we value. If we articulate a mission that focuses on student learning, yet fail to recognize and celebrate the work of students and adults when improvement occurs, they will not believe we mean our mission, and they won't believe their achievements matter. How and how often leaders publically recognize the work of individuals and groups is critically important. It is especially important to frequently and publically celebrate learning improvement by the students who struggle the most.

Effective celebrations are genuine and linked directly to the district or school's mission, vision, values, and goals—to the hard work associated with improving student learning. Effective leaders use the power of frequent and focused celebrations to shape district culture and remind everyone of their purpose, commitments, and priorities. They find multiple ways to pay tribute to those in the organization, both individuals and groups, who are the best exemplars of district values.

There is no need to make something up in order to make the faculty, staff, or students feel good. Celebrate their real accomplishments, in ways large and small. When Janel was principal at Mountain Meadow Elementary School in White River, she began a "Let the Principal Call" plan. The

> *Effective celebrations are genuine and linked directly to the district or school's mission, vision, values, and goals—to the hard work associated with improving student learning.*

idea was simply this: when a student did something particularly noteworthy, the teacher jotted it down on a note. The principal collected notes by her phone, and whenever she had a few minutes, she called the student's parents to share a positive message. It was simply amazing how much parents appreciated these quick calls. Think about it. Typically, a phone call from the school is bad news—your child is hurt, sick, not doing his or her work, or missing class or school. Frequent and meaningful celebration will not only motivate students, faculty, and staff, but will go a long way to influence parents' perceptions of the school and district. Remember, *we* are in control of the messages we send!

Reflections

District leaders must constantly and consistently remind everyone why we are doing this work—why we are implementing professional learning community concepts and practices. Importantly, they must do this in a way that communicates, "We really mean this!" and "We are going to do everything as if it were good enough for our own children." Reflect on your district's efforts to articulate and embed a learning mission in your district's culture.

Individually or in teams, reflect on questions such as the following.

1. What processes were utilized to clarify high levels of learning as the fundamental purpose of schools in your district or school?

2. What has been done to communicate the moral purpose of the work that is being undertaken? Are the faculty and staff constantly and consistently reminded of the moral purpose of ensuring high levels of learning for all students? How?

3. What efforts have been made to embed the learning mission into the daily culture of your district and schools in your district?

4. What are some next steps that need to be taken in order to embed the learning mission deeper into the district's culture?

5. What processes were used to collaboratively describe the district or school you would need to become in order to fulfill your fundamental purpose?

6. In what ways is the vision of your district and schools within your district being utilized?

7. Are there additional ways the vision could be utilized?

8. What processes were used to collaboratively articulate the collective commitments that would need to be made in order to achieve your district's fundamental purpose and vision? How has this been done in individual schools within your district?

9. How are shared commitments communicated and utilized?

10. How are shared commitments promoted, protected, and defended?

11. How are behaviors that are excellent examples of these shared commitments publically recognized and celebrated?

12. Are behaviors that are incongruent with these commitments confronted? How? Can you recall a specific example?

13. Has your district and schools within your district developed meaningful goals you must achieve in order to fulfill your fundamental purpose and vision of the district and schools you hope to become?

14. Are the goals monitored? How? How often?

15. In addition to goals, have indicators of progress, timelines, and targets been identified?

16. To what degree do you believe district and school goals are taken seriously versus seen as simply another thing that must be done, turned in, and then forgotten?

17. What are some ways you could improve your professional learning community foundational documents (mission, vision, values and commitments, and goals) if you revisited them?

Chapter 3

Building Shared Knowledge

Becoming a professional learning community is a difficult, complex, and incremental journey. If we are to successfully reculture schools into true professional learning communities, we must develop a shared understanding of what PLC practices look like in the day-to-day world of schools. One of the best ways to help everyone gain a deep understanding of the professional learning community concept is simply to approach the task as collectively finding out everything we can about professional learning communities and the specific practices that form the basic framework of the concept, and having deep collaborative discussions about each practice in order to clarify and add meaning. In short, clarifying what it means—and what it looks like—to function as a professional learning community is a process of collaboratively learning together.

This process of building shared knowledge requires thought, planning, redundancy, and creativity. It will require more than doing a book study, listening to a consultant, or attending a few staff development meetings. Building deep understanding requires using

> *Everyone needs to see how all of the work "fits"; otherwise, professional learning communities will just seem like one more initiative.*

multiple approaches over an extended period of time and thoroughly exploring how various PLC concepts and practices interconnect and support each other. We like to think of this process of ensuring clarity as "connecting the dots." It affects virtually every aspect of how things are done across the entire school district. Everyone needs to see how all of the work "fits"; otherwise, professional learning communities will just seem like one more initiative.

Faculty and staff also need to have a sense of urgency to learn more about the professional learning community concept and practices in meaningful ways. Now is the time for district leaders to communicate the firm decision that professional learning communities is the approach the district will take to improve learning across the district. It is not one of many ways. It is *the* way! This is where the district has chosen to put its effort, time, and resources. District leaders must clearly communicate that they are not going to "dance around" this "learning thing" anymore, and there will be no more fad du jour or the flavor of the month initiatives. All district leaders must speak with one voice to consistently deliver the same message.

Start at the Top

It is impossible to develop a deep understanding of professional learning community practices throughout the district unless district leaders have first gained a deep knowledge base themselves. We must remember the PLC way of thinking will be new to most people. So, in effect, leaders must learn and lead at the same time.

As the work of implementing professional learning community practices gets underway, faculty and staff will often need a go-to person—someone who can explain what is going on and why the work is important. It is critically important that those in leadership positions be out front in acquiring a deep understanding of the professional learning community concept. District leaders are going to be called on to answer questions, to clarify, and to add meaning. They must be prepared, confident, and capable of providing accurate information. If they are not confident in their own knowledge and understanding, they will never be able to build confidence in those around them. In short, leaders must be at least as knowledgeable as the people they are attempting to lead.

> *The need to build a strong guiding coalition composed of leaders representing various groups from across the district cannot be overemphasized.*

In order to ensure that every administrator hears the same message, we suggest the district conduct workshops for district administrators with a focus on "What Is a Professional Learning Community, and How Does It Work?" We believe it is critically important to begin with the district leadership. Importantly, we also urge school board members to attend these workshops and become strong supporters of district efforts to utilize professional learning community practices to improve learning across the district. We also always recommend building a guiding coalition of leaders, especially teacher leaders, from across the district.

This districtwide learning improvement team, usually assembled by the superintendent, can explore a systemwide approach to improve learning by implementing professional learning community practices in every school, team, and classroom within the district.

The need to build a strong guiding coalition composed of leaders representing various groups from across the district cannot be overemphasized. A guiding coalition that has learned about and discussed in deep and meaningful ways the practices that form the framework of the PLC concept can be a powerful tool. Reculturing an entire school district is a huge endeavor, and beginning with everyone at the same time only leads to confusion, misunderstanding, and quite often, resistance. It is much better to reap the benefits of first working with a smaller group to build shared knowledge, work through issues, and build allies before engaging the entire faculty and staff within the district. We often use the military analogy of establishing and securing a beachhead before moving out. And, of course, the guiding coalition members should not only be seen as allies but as a core group of leaders who can be a valuable resource as building shared knowledge is incrementally undertaken throughout the district.

Start at the Bottom, Too

In chapter 1, we highlighted the importance of leaders acting on the assumption that implementing professional learning community practices must be both top down and bottom up. Therefore, one of the first things we urge districts to do, as we did in the White River School District, is to align leadership behavior with this critical assumption. A key aspect of being a leader who gets it is knowing what you don't know—accepting the fact that no single person will know all the answers to everything. Leaders must shift from a mindset of "I must know how to do everything and solve all issues," to one of "we will seek out best practices, seek help from others, learn together, and work together in a culture of continuous improvement." Effective leaders approach all issues by first gaining *shared* knowledge.

> *Leaders must shift from a mindset of "I must know how to do everything and solve all issues," to one of "we will seek out best practices, seek help from others, learn together, and work together in a culture of continuous improvement."*

This shift means not only sharing knowledge about PLC top down but also letting existing knowledge flow from the bottom up. In many districts, there is already at least one school where student achievement levels far exceed all the others—one school that causes the district office to ask, "How is this school getting such great results? We know people there say they are functioning as a professional learning community, but what does that mean—what are they doing?" Accordingly, the guiding coalition should look for evidence of successful professional learning community practices that are already in place.

In White River, that exemplary school was Mountain Meadow Elementary. Mountain Meadow was absolutely committed to a focus on learning for all students by implementing professional learning community practices. Incrementally, Mountain Meadow made tremendous gains in student achievement, clearly outperforming other elementary schools in the White River School District and in surrounding districts as well.

For example, as the data in table 3.1 indicate, in 1999, Mountain Meadow students were struggling in math and reading, and in writing, only 19 percent were demonstrating proficiency. Each year the student learning levels improved to the point that by 2006, almost 90 percent of the students were demonstrating proficiency in math and writing, and 96 percent were meeting proficiency levels in reading.

Table 3.1: Mountain Meadow Student Progress, 1999–2006

Skill Area	1999	2000	2001	2002	2003	2004	2005	2006
Math	43.1	56.1	66.2	65.2	81.4	92.5	83.9	86.5
Reading	68.4	84.8	79.2	76.6	78.6	98.1	90.3	96.0
Writing	19.0	43.9	64.9	59.1	68.6	77.4	88.7	88.7

These results quite naturally led district leaders to ask what Mountain Meadow did to embed PLC practices and how they were getting such impressive results. The logical next question was whether the work educators were doing at Mountain Meadow could be equally effective throughout the district.

In our work across North America, we have found the White River example to be more common than we expected. District reculturing is often fueled by one school—or even one or two teams within a school—that is implementing professional learning community practices, getting tremendous results, and thus becoming a catalyst for others. District leaders who search out and examine best practices within their own district achieve two results: they honor the hard work of those who are already experiencing success, and they reinforce the districtwide perception that PLC practices offer the best hope for sustained school improvement.

Effective district leaders recognize, however, that having one or two schools standing alone as islands of excellence is simply unacceptable. The challenge is the same as the one facing all school districts—how to ensure high levels of learning in every school, for every student, throughout the entire district. In the White River School District the constant focus was, How can we make every school, every classroom, and every lesson good enough for our own children?

Read, Discuss, Train

Being a professional carries with it the implication that our behavior is based on the latest and best knowledge available at any given point in the time. To fulfill the mission and vision of professional learning communities, the learning improvement team, whatever it is called, in each district should begin by examining research on best practices and then leading collaborative discussion around the findings. The first step is always to learn together to gain shared knowledge about topics such as effective leadership, organizational practices, collaborative teaming, and effective teaching strategies—to name but a few.

As the guiding coalition members begin to gain a deeper understanding and appreciation for the potential of the professional learning community concepts to improve student learning, they frequently take the lead in informing others within and throughout the district. Administrators, particularly principals, should be provided with materials and resources to use not only for their own learning but for building staff knowledge in their schools. We regularly recommend that district leaders make articles available to faculty and staff and that the implications of the points in the articles be collaboratively discussed in small-group settings.

If we want faculty and staff to gain a deep understanding and context for PLC concepts and practices and, ultimately, do the hard work of district and school reculturing, we have an obligation to provide them with high-quality, relevant resources.

The quality of resources we provide faculty and staff matters! If we want faculty and staff to gain a deep understanding and context for PLC concepts and practices and, ultimately, to do the hard work of district and school reculturing, we have an obligation to provide them with high-quality, relevant resources. High-quality, relevant books, videos, workshops, conferences, and consultants can help clarify the work of a professional learning community. The appendix includes an annotated list of resources ("Getting Started," page 211) that we've found helpful.

One thing that will quickly become apparent is that the phrase *learning community* is used to describe a wide variety of educational initiatives. As we mentioned earlier, schools that call themselves PLCs are much more prevalent than schools that really function as PLCs. The more successful districts with which we have worked quickly rule out practices that are incorrectly described as the professional learning community concept. We urge leaders to provide faculty and staff with accurate, meaningful, and relevant information—especially successful examples—about professional learning community concepts and practices.

Develop a Common Vocabulary

Shared knowledge is built on more than mere definitions, but let's face it, words matter—a lot! Building shared knowledge requires a purposeful clarification of words, phrases, concepts, and, importantly, rationale. Terms and phrases such as *shared values and commitments, collaborative teams, team norms, common formative assessments,* and *time, support, and enrichment* form the routine language of schools that function as professional learning communities, yet may be interpreted very differently through the lens of individual experience and knowledge.

Each of the words *professional, learning,* and *community* implies a number of important assumptions. Everyone must understand what each of these words means and the implications each has for how we can best ensure all students—and adults—learn at high levels. For example, as we noted earlier, *professional* implies a number of things, but one important implication is that the work of professionals—what they do—should be based on the latest and best knowledge. This assumption has tremendous implications for district culture and the expectation that our attempts to improve should always begin by engaging in collective inquiry.

> *We must continually communicate the implications the learning mission has for specific practices at the district, school, team, teacher, and student levels.*

The word *learning* communicates the significance of the district's passionate and intense focus on its core mission—that its fundamental purpose is to ensure high levels of learning for all students and that student learning is significantly impacted by the quality of adult learning. This cultural shift from an emphasis on ensuring that state standards were taught to ensuring that the essential outcomes were learned is the foundation for other practices that form the professional learning community framework. We must continually communicate the implications the learning mission has for specific practices at the district, school, team, teacher, and student levels. Think of it this way: when students return home after a day at school, parents ask, "What did you learn today?" not "What were you taught?"

The word *community* recognizes the fact that the district cannot achieve its mission of ensuring high levels of learning for all students if faculty and staff continue to work in isolation. Highly effective collaborative teaming must become the "way we do things" across the entire district.

As important as it is that everyone gains a deep, rich understanding of the implications of the words *professional learning community*, it is equally important to clarify the meaning of a whole host of words that are routinely used as part of the professional learning communities lexicon—words such as *mission, vision, values, SMART goals, power standards, essential outcomes, common formative assessments, summative assessments, collective inquiry, pyramid of interventions,* and others. Repeated efforts must be made to ensure a deep understanding of a common vocabulary that will be used throughout the district. For a more in-depth treatment of this topic, see "Key Terms and Concepts in a PLC" in *Revisiting Professional Learning Communities at Work* (DuFour et al., 2008).

Connect the Dots

Keep in mind, deep reculturing of a school district involves changing virtually everything and everyone—people's assumptions, attitudes, knowledge base, and most importantly, behaviors. As teams begin working together to implement PLC practices, they often ask, "Where does this fit?" District leaders should use every opportunity to clarify where various practices fit by constantly putting them in the context of the four critical questions of learning (DuFour, DuFour, Eaker, & Many, 2010):

1. What do we want students to learn?
2. How will we know if they've learned it?
3. What will we do if they haven't learned it?
4. What will we do if they've demonstrated proficiency?

It is essential to illustrate the *interconnectedness* of the critical questions related to learning. For example, everyone must understand that it is impossible to write high-quality common formative assessments unless teams first clarify the essential outcomes students are expected to learn—the outcomes they will be assessed on. Similarly, it is impossible to plan appropriate time and support or enrichment for students unless the school creates an effective way to monitor student learning on a frequent and timely basis. The most successful districts with which we have worked emphasized the four critical questions of learning with planned, persistent redundancy.

It is also important to continually present PLC practices in the context of the big picture. For example, one teacher in White River remarked, "I just don't understand. Last year the principal had each grade-level team identify the essential outcomes in each subject. Then she asked us to begin writing and analyzing the results of common assessments, and now the principal is talking about the importance of developing a schoolwide plan for additional time, support, and enrichment for students. I just don't see where all of this fits!" What this teacher needed was simply for someone to take the time to pull up a chair and explain how the four critical questions of learning are interconnected and interdependent. The quality of a team's work around one critical question will depend on the quality of the work it does around the other questions.

Additionally, district leaders must, at every opportunity, connect the work back to the district's mission of ensuring high levels of learning for all students. If we aren't careful, some faculty and staff will view implementing the professional learning community concept as the district's goal, rather than as a proven, commonsense *approach to achieving* our real goal of helping all students learn more. Help everyone understand how the professional learning community concept connects and impacts virtually every aspect of district and school culture. Everyone will be called on to examine his or her own beliefs and practices under the light of the district's learning mission and the research-based best practices that inform a professional learning community. Everything—district meetings and agendas, the development of policies, budgeting, professional development, hiring, performance appraisal, technology, curriculum, instruction, materials and resources, school schedules, assessment, student support services, and district and school community relations—everything must be connected to the district mission of ensuring high levels of learning. District leaders must constantly and consistently point out and emphasize these connections.

Provide Extra Time and Support for Adult Learning

Despite our very best and repeated attempts to explain and clarify what professional learning communities are and how they work, a few people will take longer to understand the idea, even at the most basic level. The following comment is typical of those that demonstrate this lack of understanding. In August 2007, before the school year began (the second year of implementing PLC practices in White River), a teacher was playing golf with the high school principal. As they were walking along, the teacher asked, "So, are we going to be doing that PLC thing again next year?"

The principal's reply emphasized that yes, they were going to continue to make sure they knew what they wanted students to learn, and they were going to continue to monitor the learning of students and provide them with additional time and support when they experienced difficulty. Yes, their school was going to continue to focus on the learning of their students. In short, they would continue to do their job!

This pattern has proven to be true in every district with which we have worked—adults, like students, learn at different rates and in different ways. We like to think of the district, in fact, as just a bigger classroom. As leaders we will have to differentiate our teaching methods, and we'll need formative assessments along the way to check for understanding on a frequent and timely basis. We'll reteach, monitor, adjust, and continually provide timely, systematic, and direct additional time, support, and enrichment for teams as well as for individuals. Often, just like good teachers, we'll have a one-on-one dialogue with a person who does not understand and teach them in a deep, rich way. We'll discuss this more in chapter 7 on ensuring adult learning.

The point is this: we cannot assume that just because we have done a thorough job explaining that faculty and staff have, in fact, learned. Districts must approach clarifying the professional learning community concept with a relentless redundancy of message—a constant and consistent drip, drip, drip! We'll explore how to do this in greater depth in the following chapters.

> *Districts must approach clarifying the professional learning community concept with a relentless redundancy of message—a constant and consistent drip, drip, drip!*

Refuse to Settle for *PLC Lite*

In virtually every district with which we have worked, there are also a few people who settle for *professional learning communities lite*—simply doing enough to get by, picking and choosing the PLC practices they want to do or feel comfortable doing. For example, some principals might attend meetings, but not become engaged in deep, sincere ways. Even though they are in physical attendance, mentally they are somewhere else. Imagine, then, how much clarity and enthusiasm these principals show when they attempt to explain professional learning community practices and concepts to their faculties.

In addition to insisting that everyone participate in the PLC process, district leaders must continually send the message that they will not settle for teams doing bits and pieces of the work associated with improving student learning. Professional learning community practices only have power as a whole. And ultimately, the best way to help faculty and staff gain a deep, rich understanding of professional learning community concepts and practices is by *actually doing the work* of a professional learning community. This is the only way educators can gain confidence in the power of the professional learning community concept and practices—and in their own ability—to effectively improve student learning. Most important, it is the only way to get true buy-in. We've learned there is not much we can say on the front end that will convince faculty and staff in the power of the professional learning community concept to impact student learning. But when the data show that more kids are learning more, then faculty and staff become believers.

Motivate and Inspire

Simply implementing PLC practices is never enough. District leaders who seek to reculture their districts into high-performing professional learning communities must do so with a sense of passion and excitement. Faculty and staff will feel just as much excitement and optimism as their leaders show, and that sense of excitement and promise affects attitudes every single day. Leaders must introduce the professional learning community concept with passion, persistence, excitement, and energy. Effective leaders help everyone realize "the data are us" by connecting what we are doing with the names and faces of our kids.

What We Have Learned About Building Shared Knowledge

As the faculty and staff expand their shared knowledge by reading books, watching videos, attending institutes, discussing best practice and student data, and doing the work of a professional learning community, questions and misconceptions will emerge. District leaders need to be proactive and creative in providing clarification at every level. Consider some of the following strategies White River used to reinforce shared knowledge throughout the district.

PLC Emails

Anticipating that the faculty and staff would continue to have numerous questions (and misconceptions), the Deputy Superintendent for Teaching and Learning in White River sent an email approximately every six weeks to everyone in the school district, including the support staff, to clarify a particular PLC issue or practice. In addition to clearing up misunderstandings and misconceptions, these emails became an important tool for:

- Creating a common vocabulary
- Building a deeper understanding of professional learning community practices and concepts

- Communicating how and why the practices were being embedded into district culture
- Showing how various practices connected with each other
- Keeping everyone updated on what was being done at each level across the district
- Sharing the next step of the work

By including everyone in the email dialogue, the entire faculty and both certified and noncertified staff, the district explicitly declared that everyone, regardless of job title, played an important role enhancing student learning—everyone mattered. There was another, unintended benefit to sending the emails to all: everyone who read them was able to explain to the larger community what was happening in the district and why it was important. Shared through the faculty and staff, the emails served as an important information link to the larger White River community.

One of the first emails addressed questions from an increasing number of faculty and staff: "Why are we doing this? What research shows that professional learning communities truly make a difference?" This email made an enormous difference in how the faculty and staff viewed the work they were being asked to do.

However, it also became increasing clear that some faculty and staff viewed the professional learning community concept as a program. So, another districtwide email explained that the district's mission—its core purpose—was to ensure high levels of student learning and that the professional learning community concept was simply a way of thinking about effective practices as the district went about the task of fulfilling its mission. Later emails addressed specific questions, such as those from support staff asking, "Why do we have to attend these meetings?" and "What is our role in all of this professional learning community work?"

When a district functions as a professional learning community, everything is affected, either directly or indirectly. Everyone is asked to think and, more important, to *behave* in new and different ways. White River's districtwide emails proved to be an effective way for helping all faculty and staff understand that, although they may have different job titles and responsibilities, they share a singular purpose—to help the district in its mission to ensure high levels of learning for all students. Because of the positive effect the emails had in the White River district, we urge each district with which we work to embrace the practice. Samples are included in the appendix for many of the issues discussed in this book. See page 163 for the email on "Professional Learning Communities as a Way of Thinking" and page 167 for the email on "The Role of Support Staff in a Professional Learning Community."

Writing It Down

One of the things district leaders in White River began to realize as a result of the PLC emails was just how much faculty and staff appreciate receiving information in writing. We urge district administrators to answer questions in writing and to share questions and answers with others beyond the original exchange. The fact is, when we respond in writing, we give more thought to our answer than we do when responding casually in conversation with an off-the-top-of-the-head response. If one person has a question, others probably have the same question. Provide answers that faculty and staff can easily share with each other.

Putting things in writing also helps reduce gossip. Too often, simply telling one person something becomes a game of telephone; the answer to a question becomes skewed and loses all meaning as it's repeated from person to person throughout the school or district. Proactive communications and responses in writing go a long way in promoting clear, concise, and accurate communication.

The Learning Letter

Typically, newsletters are simply that—announcements about news. Most districts regularly distribute some kind of newsletter throughout the district and the larger community on a regular basis. In addition to the more traditional newsletter, White River developed a "learning letter" to faculty and staff. Learning letters were also placed on the district's website, which served to inform the larger community. The learning letter provides an additional vehicle for clarifying purpose, practices, and terms, as well as for addressing common questions, myths, and misconceptions. It's also the perfect place to highlight the hard work and successes of individuals and teams—particularly student achievement gains as they begin to surface. (A sample learning letter from White River appears on page 188.)

Board Learning Meetings

It would be difficult to overstate the importance of working effectively with the school board as efforts to reculture the district are underway. Most school districts leave it to the superintendent to explain and clarify initiatives to the school board. At White River, the Superintendent and the Deputy Superintendent for Teaching and Learning worked tirelessly to ensure the board was fully informed, but they realized that board members would value insights from faculty and staff (as well as students). They also realized that in order for board members to respond to community questions and concerns, board members would need to be continually learning about how professional learning community practices were being embedded into the White River culture.

To assist the board in gaining a deeper understanding, the district began holding an additional "board learning meeting" each month. At these meetings, principals, teacher teams, support staff, or students shared what they were doing as White River focused on improving student learning. These meetings were informal and typically involved a brief presentation and examples and evidence of the work being done, followed by questions and deep, rich dialogue. Stories from the faculty and staff were particularly informative. For example, at one meeting Judy B., a teacher, told the board she had thought of her entire career as a teacher in White River as the "wonder years": "I wonder what that teacher is doing. I wonder how she gets such good results." Judy commented that it was only when she became part of a high-performing collaborative team that she felt an awareness beyond her classroom. Teacher after teacher shared similar stories.

Since board meetings were covered by the local press, the newspaper articles that appeared after each meeting proved to be a helpful addition to the district's efforts to educate and inform the White River community. Board members were able to walk away from these meetings with a clearer understanding of not only what was being done and why it was being done but, importantly, how faculty and staff felt about it. This enabled the board to communicate with others more clearly. Because of the success White River had with its board learning meetings, we urge other districts to adopt a similar strategy.

Community Outreach

The culture of a school district extends beyond the central office and individual schools. It also is affected by how district leaders communicate with parents and the larger community. District leaders must take steps to ensure that virtually everything they do communicates a commitment to improving student learning.

For example, in the White River School District, something as routine as the Back-to-School Night was redesigned to align with and communicate the focus on student learning. Rather than the traditional review of classroom rules, how to volunteer, and so on, the new Back-to-School Night focused on such things as sharing essential learning standards with parents, clarifying what the standards mean, and explaining what they look like in student work. Teachers explained their expectations regarding homework, as well as the conditions in which students would be required to redo work. Most important, they communicated how students would receive additional time, support, and enrichment.

Here's another example: the math department at White River High School held a Geometry Parent Night. Teachers discussed the standards, described the support that was available to students and specific ways parents could help, provided parents with hands-on opportunities to use online resources, and addressed parent questions and concerns. Over one hundred parents showed up! White River High School also held an Advanced Placement Parent Night for parents of students who were enrolled in advanced placement courses. Again, a significant number of parents gathered to learn how they could support their children and their learning. The fact is, a community will learn by our *actions* what we really, deep down, *believe*.

Sharing Beyond the District

As White River began to experience success in improving student achievement and acquire a reputation of excellence, administrators and faculty were increasingly asked to visit neighboring districts to share what they were doing to reculture their district into a professional learning community. Additionally, faculty and staff in White River began to publish articles in state and national journals and speak at state, regional, and national meetings.

These efforts to inform others served three important purposes. First, it forced those who were presenting and writing to clarify and sharpen their own understanding of professional learning community concept and related practices. Second, the articles became an additional way to inform others within the district as well as a larger audience of professional learning community practices. Third, faculty and staff began to take pride in the fact that others were looking to them as an exemplary model. This sense of pride served as important motivator to drill deeper—to continuously get better.

Celebrate, Celebrate, Celebrate

It is impossible to overstate the importance of frequent, meaningful celebrations for both students and adults. All organizations celebrate what is most valued, and in the absence of public recognition and celebrations, things we declare as important will lose all meaning. Additionally, public recognition, rituals, and ceremonies serve to keep the spark of enthusiasm alive. The journey to creating a professional learning community has no end, because our goal is to ensure that all students are learning at high levels. The question, then, is, How do you maintain a sense of excitement and energy for a journey that is never completed?

The answer is through frequent and meaningful celebrations. Celebrations are fun! They are the flip side, the earned counterpart to the hard work that must be done incrementally over time, day by day. Remember, effective leadership touches the emotions, and public recognition that celebrates the accomplishments of both individuals and groups is an essential tool in every effective leader's toolbox.

Celebrations don't have to be elaborate or costly, but they must be tied directly to those milestones that are reached along the way—either when students demonstrate that they are learning more or when adults complete difficult and complex tasks that are tied directly to the mission, vision, or values and commitments of the district, school, or team.

Reflections

It is critical that we clarify and add meaning to concepts and practices we hope to implement districtwide. This is especially true of the professional learning community concept since, if fully implemented, professional learning community practices will be pervasive across the entire school district, affecting virtually every aspect of district culture.

Individually or in teams, reflect on questions such as the following.

1. What actions have been taken in your school or district to ensure that everyone has a deep, rich understanding of PLC concepts and practices?

2. To what degree does everyone understand what professional learning communities are, how they work, and how they differ from more traditional schools? How do you know they understand?

3. To what degree do faculty and staff understand that the professional learning community concept is simply a means to an end, and that the end is the moral purpose of ensuring high levels of learning for all students? How do you know they understand?

4. Are there additional actions to build shared knowledge that you think should be taken? If so, what are they?

5. Was there a collaborative effort to gain shared knowledge regarding the research on effective schools and school districts, as well as the research on leadership, effective organizations, and collaborative teaming? How was this done? How effective was it?

6. What resources have been used to help faculty and staff understand professional learning community concepts and practices?

7. Have you received high-quality examples of the kind of work that needs to be accomplished?

8. What additional resources do you think might be useful?

9. Does the school or district continually reinforce the fundamental ideas that form the framework of the PLC concept? How?

10. What tools (handouts, videos, newsletters, and so on) have been created to communicate the learning mission of your district? What additional tools might be helpful?

11. Do things frequently take precedence over best practices associated with promoting student learning, despite the learning mission? How does this happen? Why? How might this avoided, or at least significantly reduced?

Chapter 4

Aligning Policies, Practices, and Procedures With the Learning Mission

It is not enough to simply declare a mission of ensuring high levels of learning for all students and build shared knowledge about PLC terms and practices. This fundamental purpose must be aligned with and embedded into the policies and procedures that drive daily work throughout the district—not just of teachers, but of administrators as well.

Unfortunately, it's not uncommon for districts and schools to declare a learning mission and then continue to utilize outdated policies, practices, and procedures that are incongruent with that mission. Successful PLC districts move beyond merely recognizing the importance of alignment and engage in a systematic, collaborative, critical review of each policy, procedure, and practice to *ensure* alignment. Effective district leaders examine every decision through this learning lens, asking, "What is the probable impact on learning?" They work to shift organizational culture from one of random, hurried decision making to one of thoughtful, learning-focused decision making.

> *Effective district leaders examine every decision through this learning lens, asking, "What is the probable impact on learning?"*

District leaders do this by first modeling and protecting the focus on learning. These leaders:

- Communicate the expectations for key positions to achieve the learning mission
- Define how quality of performance will be measured in relation to the expectations
- Communicate how the district will assist efforts to improve performance in relation to the expectations
- Demonstrate how exemplary performance will be celebrated

Notice that these points parallel the four critical questions for student learning: What do we want students to know? How will we know when they've learned it? What will we do when they don't learn? How will we respond when they exceed expectations? (DuFour, DuFour, Eaker, & Many, 2010). Let's examine how this alignment work can be done.

Model and Protect the Focus on Learning

It is incredibly difficult to keep student learning at the very center of what we do. One of the most important cultural shifts a district can make is to refocus the district's own work on learning—to parallel and model what the district expects from teachers in the classroom. For example, most district leaders want their teachers to move from focusing on low-level memorization of facts to promoting higher levels of thinking, such as analyzing, synthesizing, and evaluating. Yet often in meetings, what do administrators do? Focus on low-level communication. Meetings are constantly in danger of degenerating into traditional, low-level information exchanges. Not only is this an inefficient use of time, it's a misuse of limited resources. The combined salaries of everyone who attends a meeting of central office personnel and building principals is very significant—so significant, in fact, that administrators should spend that time discussing important, complex, and relevant issues! Rethink how you can accomplish the routine communications more efficiently (perhaps using technology), and save the majority of face-to-face meeting time for deeper, more significant discussions related to improving student learning.

Let everyone see that the same expectations are held for district and faculty meetings as for collaborative team meetings. Effective leaders do not allow other things to trump the district's fundamental mission. Although there is always pressure at district meetings to discuss nuts-and-bolts items ("I need a few minutes to talk about the issue of the Foundation Auction next week"), those items should never land at the top of the agenda. The answer should always be no or "If we do, it will have to be at the end of the agenda." What we *say* we value must be reinforced by what we *do*.

In White River, we found that even when district leaders were clear in their message that the late-start collaborative team time must focus on issues related to student learning, people often asked to put things on the agenda that had nothing to do with student learning. We knew it was critical to honor the commitment made to the board of education that if they approved the late start each Monday, the team meetings would focus on the critical questions related to improving student learning. In other words, we learned the importance of developing a culture of no.

The focus on student learning can be communicated in many small ways that add up and ultimately have an impact on district culture. In the sample agenda in figure 4.1 (page 64), for example, notice that the meeting is titled "Administrative Learning Meeting" and that the topics for discussion are organized under each of the critical questions of a professional learning community (as developed by DuFour, DuFour, Eaker & Many, 2010). Figure 4.2 (page 65) shows an agenda that requires participants to bring artifacts of student learning and reminds principals of the urgency of the mission.

District leaders have to make sure that their meetings are meaningful and will have an impact—that they do the right high-quality work. District leaders must continually focus attention on student learning. It is often the combination of seemingly little things we do that collectively sends a powerful message. Strive to be thoughtful and purposeful even in the words you choose. For example, in White River, school improvement plans came to be called "learning improvement plans." The newsletter was referred to as a *learning* letter. Again, any one of these language changes was rather insignificant, but collectively they served as a constant reminder to everyone that learning was at the core of the district culture.

District leaders also encourage their boards to continually ask the right questions—that is, "Are the kids learning?" and "How do we know?" Even in times of tough budget cuts, school boards must filter their decisions by asking, "How can we balance the budget, but at the same time fulfill our moral purpose?" After all, what could possibly take precedence over the learning needs of a community's own children? At White River, the questions, What would this look like if we really meant it? and Is this good enough for my own child? became important filters for our discussions and decisions. To ensure meetings wouldn't deteriorate into meaningless routines, agendas always include these two questions. They truly became the quality filters of our time together.

Four Critical Questions of a PLC

1. What do we want each student to learn?
2. How will we know if each student is learning it?
3. How will we respond when a student is experiencing difficulty with learning it?
4. How will we respond if the student already knows it?

Administrative Learning Meeting
November 3rd 12:30—3:00

Question One: What do we want each student to learn?

Revisit chapter 1 from *Seven Strategies for Assessment for Learning*

Learning Targets: Please come to the meeting prepared to share actual examples of how learning targets are being used in your building. You will be placed at a table to share your examples with an administrator and Building Learning Coordinator from each level.

Learning Targets: Wilkeson Elementary School Team

Graduation Requirements: Mike Hagadone

Question Two: How will we know if each student is learning it?

SOAR (Student On-line Assessment Resource): Meagan

Question Three: How will we respond when students experience difficulty?

High School Team report on PBIS (Positive Behavior Intervention Supports) Action Plan

Other Information

Education Foundation Auction: Auction items and artists

Crucial Conversations book study

Principal Training and New Technology System

December 1st meeting

Crafting the new District Learning Improvement Plan: This will be an all-day meeting, 9:00–2:30. Each principal will need to bring your Building Learning Coordinator and two parents.

Reminders

Data meeting December 15th at Foothills Elementary School

Figure 4.1: Sample learning-focused administrative meeting agenda.

Source: White River School District. Used with permission.

What's the Impact on Learning?
Administrative Learning Meeting Agenda

Date: January 12, 2009
To: Principals
From: Janel Keating, Deputy Superintendent
Re: Principal's meeting: January 12, 3:00–4:30 p.m.

> "Leaders of PLCs must consistently communicate, through their words and actions, their conviction that the people in their school or district are capable of accomplishing great things through their collective efforts."—DuFour, DuFour, Eaker, & Many (*Learning by Doing*)

- Words of Wisdom regarding math (Janis)
- Principal's role to improve math instruction, results, and commitments
- Protocol for analyzing math assessments
- K-registration March 18th
- Training ahead (John)

You will need to bring:

You need to bring student data from a math assessment.

Elementary: Please bring a completed assessment sheet from Bridges. We need to see how each kid in the class did on specific items on the assessment. If you have questions, please call.

Middle level and high school: Please bring the assessment results from at least one math class. We need to be able to see how each student scored on each item on the assessment. Once again, let me know if you have any questions.

Do we have the will to do it?

Figure 4.2: Sample learning-focused administrative meeting agenda.

Source: White River School District. Used with permission.

Ensure a Tight Framework

District and school policies are perhaps the primary way to communicate and reinforce the things we are tight about, and at the same time they are a way to encourage experimentation and autonomy within those parameters. We view district policies much like the frame of a house, within which schools can move the furniture around, paint the walls, and so on with a great deal of autonomy.

The most significant tight policies should be the ones most directly associated with the learning mission.

The most significant tight policies should be the ones most directly associated with the learning mission: for example, the expectation that student learning is going to be the dominant lens through which the district views all work, or the expectation that work will be done in collaborative teams. These were non-negotiable in White River and other successful districts with which we have worked.

Policies and practices communicate what the district is tight about, and this message drives the expectations related to the day-to-day work of teams. For example, district leaders in White River constantly and clearly communicated that collaborative teams were expected to collaboratively identify, clarify, and align the essential outcomes of each subject, grade, or course with the state standards and summative assessments. Teams were expected to collaboratively develop common formative assessments designed to monitor the learning of each student in a frequent and timely manner, and teams were expected to collaboratively analyze the results of common formative assessments. Additionally, teachers were expected to share instructional practices with each other and learn from one another in order to improve the effectiveness of their own teaching practices. We'll discuss strategies and tools for this in chapters 5 and 6.

Equally important, district leaders expected each school to collaboratively develop a systematic plan for providing students with additional time, support, or enrichment within the school day, regardless of the teacher or teachers to whom they were assigned. And policies, practices, and procedures, both within the district and in schools, were aligned to reflect an intense and passionate focus on results—that is, are the students learning, and how do we know? (These findings are congruent with the findings of successful districts described by DuFour, DuFour, Eaker, and Karhanek [2010] in *Raising the Bar and Closing the Gap*.)

In holding others accountable to the learning mission, the district must constantly hold itself accountable as well. District leaders sometimes encourage teachers to do whatever it takes to help students learn at high levels, but then refuse to make the tough decisions at their level to ensure the work can be done successfully in every school. Often, the actions or inaction of district leaders convince teachers we really don't mean it when we say we'll do whatever it takes to ensure high levels of learning for all students. While each school district's journey to becoming a professional learning community will be unique, there are some things that district leaders must do to implement PLC concepts and practices throughout the district. The questions in figure 4.3 (page 68) outline expectations and can serve as a self-reflection tool as well as resource for planning next steps.

Principals also play a critical role in implementing professional learning community practices districtwide. Simply put, there are some things that principals must do, things that districts must be tight about. The questions in figure 4.4 (page 70) outline these expectations and can be used to foster discussion with principals as a group or as a self-reflection tool for enhancing the effectiveness of an individual principal.

Even when district office leaders and principals are enthusiastic and willing to do the things that are essential for reculturing the district and improve student learning in each school, they are often unsure about exactly must be done. Documents like these can help sharpen the understanding of everyone and at the same time assist in presenting the big picture—how all the behaviors align.

Align Organizational Structure

Many school districts are organized in a way best described as an incoherent, piecemeal structure that is the result of years of tinkering. We encourage district leaders to develop a deliberate and purposeful structure that will allow them to more clearly and efficiently focus their work of supporting and ensuring student learning.

For example, we have found that one of the most critical decisions associated with districtwide organizational structure has to do with the reporting line of principals. In many districts that have proclaimed an intense and passionate focus on ensuring all students learn at high levels, the principals still report directly to someone other than the person in the district office whose primary responsibility is teaching and learning. We urge district leaders to create an organizational structure in which principals report directly to the primary person responsible for teaching and learning. This clear line of communication reduces miscommunication and prevents principals from receiving mixed messages about priorities.

Obviously, no organizational structure is appropriate for every district. However, it is crucial every district analyze and align its organizational structure to support the district's core purpose and vision.

Clarity of Purpose

- Are district leaders absolutely clear that the fundamental purpose of the district, and everyone within the district, is to ensure high levels of learning for all students?

- Are all major decisions within the district filtered through this learning mission?

- Is there evidence of a common vocabulary and clear understanding of key terms throughout the district?

Aligning Policies, Practices, and Procedures

- Have district leaders aligned policies, practices, and procedures with the district learning mission?

- Have district leaders assisted principals in developing school schedules that allow time for collaborative teams to meet and for students to receive additional support and enrichment within the school day?

- Have district leaders aligned position descriptions and performance appraisal practices with the learning mission?

Limiting Initiatives

- Have district leaders made visible and repeated efforts to limit district initiatives?

- Are approved initiatives directly tied to the four critical questions of learning?

The Principal Principle

- Have district leaders clearly articulated the role expectations of principals?

- Is there a clear understanding that improving student learning is the primary responsibility of principals?

- Is there a clear understanding that it is the principal's responsibility to enhance the effectiveness of each team?

- Have district leaders organized principals into a collaborative team?

- Is student learning the primary focus of districtwide principal meetings?

- Does the principal team anticipate issues and questions that might arise as PLC practices are implemented?

- Do principals practice and rehearse the work that will ultimately be expected of teacher teams?

- Do principals share learning data and strategies for improvement?

Collaborative Teams

- Does the district insist that each school organize into collaborative teams?
- Have schools developed written position descriptions for the position of team leader?
- Has each school collaboratively developed criteria for the selection of team leaders?
- Does the district provide training for team leaders?

What Do Teams Do?

- Have district leaders clearly articulated what teams are expected to do and the products they are expected to produce?
- Is the work of teams tied directly to the four critical questions of learning?
- Have quality standards been collaboratively developed and articulated?
- Do district leaders provide principals and teams with training and resources they need in order to successfully do their work?

Time and Support

- Is there a clear expectation that each school will develop a system to provide students who are experiencing difficulty in their learning with additional time and support within the school day, regardless of the teacher to whom they are assigned?
- Is there a clear expectation that each school will develop a system to extend and enrich the learning of students who demonstrate proficiency?
- Does each school have a plan to monitor the effectiveness of this system?

A Focus on Results

- Is there a clear expectation from district leaders that each team (and principal) will monitor the learning of each student, skill by skill?
- Do district leaders monitor student learning on a frequent and timely basis, and are decisions made based on analysis of student learning data?

Figure 4.3: Critical questions for district office consideration.

Visit **go.solution-tree.com/plcbooks** to download a reproducible version of this figure.

Building the Foundation for a Professional Learning Community

- Has a mission of ensuring high levels of learning for all students been clearly articulated to the entire faculty, staff, students, and parents?

- Has a vision of the school you seek to become been collaboratively developed and communicated, and most important, is it being used for planning and decision making?

- Have you collaboratively developed shared commitments that all adults will adhere to in order to become the kind of school described in your vision statement? Are the commitments frequently referred to? Are they monitored? Is behavior that is incongruent with the shared commitments confronted? Are behaviors that are the best examples of the commitments publically recognized and celebrated?

- Have you collaboratively developed SMART goals for school improvement? Are they monitored?

- Have collaborative teams translated the school's SMART goals into team goals?

- Do you provide the resources and training necessary for teams to meet their SMART goals?

- Has the schedule been altered in order to provide collaborative team time within the school day?

- Does the schedule allow for students to receive additional time and support for interventions and enrichment within the school day, regardless of the teacher to whom they are assigned?

- Have policies, practices, and procedures been analyzed and aligned with your learning mission?

- Are major decisions filtered through the question, What will be the probable impact on learning?

Collaborative Teams

- Have you organized your school into collaborative teams? What plans have been made for singletons?

- Did you give great care and thought into choosing team leaders?

- Have you clearly defined the role of team leaders—in writing?

- Have you provided training for team leaders?

- Do you have regularly scheduled meetings with your team leaders in which you model how teams should work in your school?

- Have you reviewed the importance of team norms with your faculty and staff? What resources did you use?

- Have all teams written norms, including the team leaders' team?

- Are norms reviewed, adapted, and most important, used?

- Did teams share their norms with each other?

- What happens when norms are not being adhered to?

- Has the work of teams been clearly articulated? How is the work of teams monitored?

- How do you analyze the work of each team? How do you monitor the contributions of each team member? How do teams and team members receive the help they need when they experience difficulty or their work does not meet a high standard of quality?

A Clear and Passionate Focus on Learning

- Have collaborative teams clarified state standards in each grade or course and subject?

- Have the power standards or essential outcomes been collaboratively identified?

- Have the standards been aligned vertically?

- Have teams developed common pacing guides?

- Have teams engaged in the process of determining what each power standard, if met, would look like in student work?

- Have teams developed common scoring rubrics?

- Can team members apply the scoring rubrics consistently, with inter-rater reliability?

- Have teams agreed on the conditions under which students will take assessments?

Monitoring Student Learning

- Have teams been provided resources, training, and examples regarding the power and use of common formative assessments?

- Have all teams begun the process of writing common formative assessments?

- Are teams learning how to use the results of common formative assessments to make decisions about additional time, support, or enrichment for students, and how to learn from each other about ways to improve instructional effectiveness?

Figure 4.4: Critical questions for principal consideration. Continued➔

Visit **go.solution-tree.com/plcbooks** to download a reproducible version of this figure.

- Are teams sharing common formative assessments within the school and across the district (or other districts)?
- Are the assessment formats congruent with key summative assessments?
- Are assessments constantly being tweaked and improved?

Time, Support, and Enrichment

- Is there a schoolwide, systematic, written plan for providing students with additional time, support, or enrichment within the school day, regardless of the teacher to whom they are assigned?
- Is the plan timely and flexible, allowing students to move in and out of interventions?
- Is the plan directive rather than invitational?
- Does the school schedule accommodate the plan? If not, can it be adjusted so that it does?
- Does the plan commit to providing students who are most in need with the most help by your most experienced and competent staff?
- How is effectiveness of the plan monitored?

A Focus on Results

- Has the school developed a data analysis protocol to help teams structure their dialogue around evidence of student learning?
- Do individual teachers, teacher teams, and the principal monitor the learning of each student—student by student, skill by skill? How is this done? What happens with the information?
- Is the information used to make sure each student who is struggling receives appropriate and focused interventions?
- Are the learning data used to set SMART goals for improvement? Are the goals shared and monitored?
- Are teams provided with timely, accurate feedback regarding the quality of the work they are doing? Do you provide teams with assistance when necessary, and do you frequently and publically recognize and celebrate the work of individuals and teams when appropriate?

Figure 4.4: Critical questions for principal consideration.

Visit **go.solution-tree.com/plcbooks** to download a reproducible version of this figure.

Collaboratively Develop Position Descriptions

It is impossible to organize and align district work unless there is clarity about what people are expected to do in the first place. In addition, district leaders will find it virtually impossible to create a performance appraisal system that is aligned with the learning mission unless they first tackle the issue of clearly articulating the performance expectations associated with each position.

District leaders in White River quickly realized that an important aspect of reviewing and developing position descriptions was gaining a clear understanding of the relationship between various positions within the district. For example, many districts have instructional coaches or curriculum facilitators in each school. This raises a number of questions that need to be clarified and clearly communicated. For example, does the instructional coach report directly to the principal or to someone at the district office? What is the relationship between the instructional coach and team leaders? Another area that needs clarity is the relationship between special education teachers, the principal, and the director of special education. Who will have ultimate authority when there are honest differences of professional opinion? These are but a few examples of questions we began to address in White River with clearly articulated, collaboratively developed, position descriptions.

When revisiting current position descriptions or developing new ones, careful thought must be given to the process that will be used. Again, the first step is always to first gain shared knowledge. This may mean asking for a copy of a specific position description from another district or reading an article on what effective position descriptions look like and how they should be developed. Additionally, the position descriptions should be collaboratively developed, taking great care to include those who will be affected most. Faculty and staff anxiety can be diminished to a great degree simply by including those who will be the most directly impacted. Finally, all position descriptions should be transparent and public. The goal is to make sure everyone can see how all pieces of the personnel puzzle fit to create a structure of layered accountability with a focus on student learning.

However, a word of caution is in order. If position descriptions are too narrowly written and do not allow for professional judgment, they can be used as an excuse for not doing things that should be done. Someone might simply say, "Well, it wasn't in my job description!" Make sure that position descriptions emphasize the assumptions, commitments, and core behaviors that are expected, but at the same time emphasize that everyone is expected to do what needs to be done to promote the district's core purpose, vision, and values.

Figure 4.5 (page 74) shows a sample position description for a building learning coordinator that outlines exactly how the responsibilities align with the district's learning mission.

The position of Building Learning Coordinator is of critical importance as our district continues to sharpen its focus on improving student learning levels by implementing professional learning community practices and concepts. The educators who fill these positions will work side by side with the principal and closely with teacher teams, coordinating with the team leader. The Building Learning Coordinator will report directly back to the building principal.

The primary function of this position is to **enhance student learning** in the assigned building. To this end, candidates must have a **demonstrated record of exceptional teaching skills as reflected in the learning levels of their students, as well as the recognition and respect of their peers.** Simply put, each Building Learning Coordinator must be widely viewed as an exceptional teacher and command the respect of those with whom he or she will work. The Building Learning Coordinator's professional behavior must support all aspects of the district direction.

The Building Learning Coordinator will work with teacher teams to review student learning data, analyze student work, lead teams in reflective practice, share with individual teachers and teams proven best practices for enhancing student learning, and assist teams in setting and achieving learning-based SMART goals. **The Building Learning Coordinator will ensure that teams focus on the critical questions of learning in a manner reflective of the highest quality.**

Building Learning Coordinators will also focus on **improving the effectiveness of each team.** Recognizing that teams, like students, learn at different rates and in different ways, Building Learning Coordinators will model differentiated teaming, much like teachers who successfully implement differentiated instruction in classrooms. Building Learning Coordinators must understand how effective teams function and how to enhance the capacity of teams. In short, Building Learning Coordinators working side by side with their principal and are responsible for **helping each team function more efficiently and effectively.**

Recognizing that professional development in a school that functions as a professional learning community differs significantly from more traditional schools, the Building Learning Coordinator will **work with each team to assess the professional development needs and assist the principal in developing a professional development plan for the school.** The principal will then present the school's needs and plans for professional development to the Deputy Superintendent for Teaching and Learning.

Building Learning Coordinators must demonstrate leadership skills. These include the ability to facilitate groups of adult learners, build relationships with the building staff, and manage conflict when necessary to move the group forward. Excellent technology and interpersonal skills are essential. Building Learning Coordinators must work well with others, possessing the skills to work with a variety of groups and individuals, while at the same time demonstrating results. They must be a model for adult learning, constantly seeking out best practices in teaching and learning. Simply put, Building Learning Coordinators must be students of teaching.

Figure 4.5: Sample collaboratively developed, learning-aligned position description for a Building Learning Coordinator.

Source: White River School District. Used and adapted with permission.

Visit **go.solution-tree.com/plcbooks** to download a reproducible version of this figure.

Communicate Expectations During Hiring

An effective PLC district makes a concerted effort to embed the mission of ensuring high levels of learning for all students across the entire district—in every school, every team, and every classroom. While everyone plays an important role in achieving this mission, few would question the critical role the building principal plays in this endeavor.

Anyone who has studied the effective schools research of the past thirty years recognizes the critical role the principal plays in highly effective schools. Thirty-five years of effective schools research has consistently emphasized the critical importance of the building principal. The importance of the principalship poses a critical question: What should district leaders do in order to increase the odds that they will employ high-quality leaders when filling principalship positions?

One of the things they do is to give great thought and planning into the interview process of prospective candidates for the position. In spite of the critical importance of the interview for both parties and the seriousness with which interviews are conducted, there are no guarantees. Mistakes are often made. Either one party, or both, might not present an accurate picture of themselves. Sometimes it's just not the right fit! While there is no right way to conduct interviews for the principalship position, it certainly requires forethought and planning.

Effective districts adopt a new way of thinking about interviewing candidates to increase the likelihood of success. We believe we need to start hiring superintendents who were outstanding principals and principals who were outstanding teachers—who got results with the kids in their classrooms. We need to hire principals who have already been effective team members. If a person didn't get results as a teacher and wasn't a contributing member of a high-performing team, what would lead us to believe that person will get results with an entire school and be effective leading the school leadership team? It simply will not happen.

> *We believe we need to start hiring superintendents who were outstanding principals and principals who were outstanding teachers—who got results with the kids in their classrooms.*

Since principals are such a critical factor for school effectiveness, it only makes sense to give careful consideration to principal selection—even to the point of collaboratively developing a set of probing interview questions. Questions designed to determine how the candidate thinks and to reveal the candidate's value system are more valuable than questions designed to elicit specific right or wrong answers. Interestingly, simply engaging in the collaborative process of developing interview questions serves as a catalyst for reinforcing key PLC concepts and practices.

Before turning to the kinds of questions that could be asked during principal interviews, let's review the essential assumptions about PLC principals on which interviews should based:

1. Principals must believe that ensuring high levels of learning for all students is their primary responsibility.

2. Principals must believe in and have the ability to create a collaborative culture.

3. Principals must be able to successfully create a culture of continuous improvement and a focus on results.

4. Principals must develop strong parent and community relationships.

5. Principals must model the behavior they expect of others.

6. Principals must have the ability to motivate and inspire others.

Figure 4.6 explores, in depth, how an elementary school could outline the areas of focus, objectives, rationale, and key questions to create an interview process aligned with the district's mission, vision, values, and goals. This interview guide is used in the White River School District. All interviews are conducted in person, recognizing that the nonverbal aspects of responses are important. The rationale and nature of the questions are not shared with the candidates prior to the interview in order to elicit more spontaneous and genuine responses. Every candidate is asked every question, but the interview is not limited to the prepared questions. In fact, at their best, probing questions form the framework for deep, rich discussions with prospective candidates.

Define and Align Performance Appraisal

A district that is really serious about the mission of ensuring high levels of student learning by embedding the concepts and practices of professional learning communities throughout the district will collaboratively revise and align its performance appraisal processes.

Clearly articulated position descriptions and careful hiring allow a district to more clearly align its performance appraisal system with expected and valued behavior in a professional learning community. It has long been recognized that one of the most significant ways an organization communicates what it values is by what it monitors and assesses. A district that is really serious about the mission of ensuring high levels of student learning by embedding the concepts and practices of professional learning communities throughout the district will collaboratively revise and align its performance appraisal processes.

Area One: Maintaining a Focus on Learning for All

Objective: To determine the degree to which the candidate regards high levels of learning for all students as the core role of the building principal and to discover the conceptual framework and basic philosophy that will guide his or her decision making

Rationale: What a principal does is of critical importance, but anticipating what a candidate will do once hired is difficult. Of primary importance is the degree to which the candidate views learning as the fundamental purpose of schools and how he or she plans to embed a learning culture throughout the school.

1. Imagine a new parent is from out of state. This parent is moving to town and planning to enroll her first child into your elementary school. The visitor asks you to explain the role of the principal. How would you respond?

2. Parents often have concerns. How would you respond to this concern: "How will I know my child will be taught the state standards? What evidence will I have as a parent that my child will be taught and has learned the state standards?"

3. Respond to this scenario: as you examine student achievement data, it becomes clear that homework and grading practices are contributing to high failure rates in grades four and five. How would you approach this issue?

4. Respond to this scenario: you've heard staff commenting that they just don't have enough time to teach science and social studies. They just can't fit it in. Parents are complaining that their children aren't receiving instruction in science and social studies. Fifth-grade teachers are frustrated because the kids are unprepared to take the state science test in fifth grade. How would you approach this issue?

5. How would you respond to a parent who feels that even though her child is making very good grades, the child is under-learning?

Area Two: Creating a Collaborative Culture Utilizing High-Performing Teams

Objective: To determine the candidate's: (1) knowledge and commitment regarding utilizing collaborative teams, (2) expectations regarding what teams would be expected to do, and (3) view of the principal's role in helping teams become high-performing collaborative teams

Rationale: Creating a collaborative culture throughout an entire district depends, to a great degree, on each principal's skill at organizing his or her school into highly effective collaborative teams and then focusing those teams on answering the critical questions of learning and analyzing student work in an effort to improve their own professional practice as well as the learning of their students.

Continued➜

Figure 4.6: Sample principal interview questions aligned with a learning mission.

Visit **go.solution-tree.com/plcbooks** to download a reproducible version of this figure.

1. How would you respond to this teacher's comment: "I didn't go into teaching to be part of a collaborative team. I went into teaching to teach students. If others want to be on a team, that's fine, but just give me my students and let me teach them. Oh, by the way, my kids are missing out on instructional time during the Monday-morning late starts."

2. What do you think the fundamental problem might be in this scenario: a faculty member tells you in private that the team meetings and PLC Monday late starts are pretty much a waste of time. She states that her team really doesn't see the benefit to spending time analyzing student work. In her team meetings, teachers mainly just talk about their day or share frustrations about certain students and the new curricular materials. Team time could better be used if teachers were left on their own to grade papers and do lesson plans.

3. How would you go about helping a team that is struggling with analyzing student work and basically sees little connection between the collaborative process and improved student learning?

Area Three: Driving Continuous Improvement and a Focus on Results

Objective: To determine the degree to which the candidate is passionate and committed to developing a culture of continuous improvement and a focus on results

Rationale: In successful districts, the mission of ensuring high levels of learning for all students lies at the heart of not only how decisions are made, but how results are measured. This requires principals who are results oriented and constantly striving to improve their schools.

1. At the end of your first year as principal, what do you think would be a reasonable way to judge your effectiveness? At the end of three years?

2. How would you proceed if you overheard a teacher make the following comment to a new staff member: "You don't have to pay any attention to the team-developed SMART goals or the learning improvement plan. No one pays any attention to them. As a team, we just need to get something turned in and forget about it."

3. It has often been said that too much attention is paid to making sure students score well on high-stakes state summative assessments. How would you respond to this comment: "The teachers at this school are just teaching to the test."

Area Four: Providing and Developing Leadership

Objective: To determine (1) the candidate's commitment to strong, simultaneous loose-tight leadership; (2) the candidate's understanding of which things leaders should be tight about and when leaders should encourage empowerment, autonomy, and experimentation; (3) the candidate's potential to shape school culture, motivate, and inspire

Rationale: The quality of principal leadership is a key factor in school effectiveness, and the principalship is a key leadership position within the district. In the absence of high-quality leadership at the building level, critical district initiatives are destined to failure. Also, the role of the building principal is so complex and principals are responsible for so much, it is virtually impossible for even the hardest-working principal to be successful working alone. Therefore, principals must understand, believe in, and have the skills to disperse the leadership function throughout the building, especially by enhancing the role of team leader.

1. Consider this scenario: you are having an informal dinner with a group of fellow principals, and the conversation centers on whether it is better to have strong top-down leadership or more bottom-up leadership by empowering the faculty and staff. After some initial discussion, someone in the group asks you to share your position. How would you respond?

2. A parent shares with you that he doesn't really understand much of the terminology that is used by educators. For example, he asks, "So, what is the difference between a principal who is an instructional leader and one who is a learning leader?" How would you respond?

3. It's been said that leaders monitor the things they care about the most. As principal, what would be the focus of your monitoring efforts, and how would you go about that task?

4. Respond to this scenario: a teacher visits you to complain about teachers being singled out for public recognition. The teacher makes the point that this is supposed to be a team effort, and that the principal is destroying faculty spirit by singling individual teachers out for public praise. What are your basic beliefs regarding celebrations, praise, and public recognition of students, faculty, and staff?

5. At your initial faculty meeting as the new principal, you are asked, "What kinds of things are you willing to confront individual faculty and staff about?" How would you respond?

6. How would you handle the following situation? The faculty of your school has adopted a shared commitment that states: "We will provide evidence that our students have mastered state and district standards." At the end of the second grading period, you check the grade distribution of individual teachers, and you notice that one teacher has marked 35 percent of her students as not meeting the standard.

7. A friend who happens to be a professor at an area university has asked you to speak to her graduate class in educational administration. She would like for you to make three main points on your view about leadership and then take questions. Elaborate a little on the three points you would make and why you would choose these particular points.

Continued➔

8. You have been asked by a state professional organization to write a brief article on the topic of what effective leaders do to motivate and inspire. What are some things you would be sure to include in your article?

Area Five: Building Strong Parent and Community Relations

Objective: To determine the degree the candidate will be creative and proactive in creating high-quality parent and community relationships

Rationale: A successful PLC district prides itself on its excellent parent and community relations. Additionally, study after study of effective schools points to the important role of parents in an effective school culture. The building principal plays a key role in developing the tone of these relationships as well as specific parent and community initiatives.

1. Suppose that in your first meeting with the president of the parent-teacher association, the parent shares with you that many parents feel that what the school really wants is their money and help—but not their "interference" in classrooms. What examples could you give this parent to provide reassurance that under your leadership, this school would welcome parental input and involvement?

2. In a meeting with the superintendent, you realize that the expectation within the district is for a creative and proactive approach to parent and community relations. How would you proceed in developing an exemplary program? What are some key elements in an exemplary parent and community relations program?

3. In a faculty meeting, the topic of discussion centers on involving parents in educational decisions about their children. One faculty member states, "This is an improper role of parents. It's the school's job to deal with educational issues and the parents' job to support the school's efforts." How would you respond?

Area Six: Ensuring Success

Objective: To determine the degree to which the candidate has been successful in previous roles

Rationale: Successful principals have also been highly successful in previous roles. Of particular importance is the candidate's success as a classroom teacher. There is no evidence that someone who performed in a rather mediocre way in previous roles will suddenly become a highly successful principal, if only given the opportunity. Candidates for a principal position should cite evidence beyond mere anecdotal examples when they "felt" they were successful.

1. This district holds very high expectations for building principals. What evidence and examples can you cite that would lead us to conclude that you have been highly successful in previous roles?

Area Seven: Managing Effectively

Objective: To determine (1) the candidate's understanding of the difference between leadership and management and (2) the candidate's ability and commitment to focus on both of these areas rather than choose one at the expense of the other

Rationale: While a successful district needs principals who are outstanding leaders, principals must also perform daily building tasks in a timely, high-quality manner. Principals are expected to be valuable contributing members of the district leadership team who voice concerns and opinions, yet also model the collegiality the district expects from all staff.

1. Respond to this scenario: a frequent topic in faculty meetings is the need to make sure students do their work on time and behave better. At the same time, you have noticed that many teachers are often late to staff meetings and workshops and talk to each other during the session. At one workshop you saw a teacher reading a magazine.

2. In our district, principals meet on a regular basis. One aspect of these meetings is to learn together. You have been asked to share with the group your thoughts about the difference between leadership and management. What are the basic points you would make?

3. Respond to this scenario: you are having dinner with a close friend who also happens to be a building principal. The friend confides that there simply isn't enough time to get everything done and that he has let a number of things "slide." Much of the work he turns in is late and not of the quality he would like. The friend explains that you simply have to do some things of less quality or even be late with your work if you're going to focus on the things that really matter. How would you respond? What suggestions would you offer your friend?

Figure 4.6: Sample principal interview questions aligned with a learning mission.

Visit **go.solution-tree.com/plcbooks** to download a reproducible version of this figure.

We also urge district leaders to engage in deep, rich discussions about the fundamental purpose of performance appraisal. In White River, performance appraisal is seen primarily as a tool for improving performance. We started the process of aligning our performance appraisal system with our learning mission by asking, "How can the use of this tool be improved in order to be more effective?" This led us to move from utilizing more traditional numerical rating scales to high-quality narratives. These narratives proved much more useful for describing the quality of work that was being performed throughout the district and equipping personnel to set specific improvement goals. See page 169 in the appendix for a sample performance appraisal ("Annual Administrative Performance Evaluation").

Align Professional Development

The most effective district leaders with whom we have worked thoughtfully and purposefully developed professional development plans that were designed specifically to enhance the capacity of collaborative teams to successfully impact student learning.

Although we address the issue of adult learning in a professional learning community in chapter 7 in more depth, at this point we want to emphasize the importance of aligning professional development with the district's learning mission and the work inherent in functioning as a professional learning community. It is disingenuous and unproductive to expect faculty and staff to perform at high levels, yet fail to provide them with the training and resources to be successful. The most effective district leaders with whom we have worked thoughtfully and purposefully developed professional development plans that were designed specifically to enhance the capacity of collaborative teams to successfully impact student learning.

What We Have Learned About Aligning Policies, Practices, and Procedures

If districts are to successfully fulfill their mission of ensuring high levels of learning for all students, they must focus their efforts on changing the fundamental culture of the district. However, successful systemic cultural change requires attention be paid to *structural* issues as well as cultural ones; structure and culture affect each other. We continue to gain insights on how to align district and school policies and practices with a district learning mission. Let's consider some key lessons.

Pace Yourself

A school district is a complex organization with a wide range of policies, practices, and procedures, and critically analyzing and aligning them all can seem like an overwhelming endeavor. The fact is, if you try to do them all at once, it *will* be overwhelming! Instead, review policies, practices, and procedures as you approach various tasks that must be done—review them as you do the work.

For example, when district leaders in White River needed to hire a new elementary principal, they realized that they first needed to review their hiring policies, practices, and procedures—even the interview questions that would be utilized! On the team level, as teams clarified the essential outcomes in each subject, grade, and course, they realized they also needed to review their homework, grading, and reporting practices.

This incremental approach will not only make the process seem less overwhelming, it will add a high degree of relevance to the work. For example, it is very difficult to talk about ensuring high levels of learning for all students—kid by kid, skill by skill—and not engage in deep, rich discussions about student mastery of skills, what the mastery would look like in student work, how to create common scoring rubrics, as well as the implications for a whole host of practices. This incremental approach also enhances the efforts to do the work with a high degree of quality.

Institutionalize Your Core Purpose

As districts begin to review their policies, practices, and procedures, an issue that quickly comes to the forefront is what they should be absolutely tight about. Policies and procedures should be viewed as the framework within which everyone will operate. In other words, they are the essential first step in institutionalizing a district's core purpose—ensuring student learning. To fulfill that commitment, district leaders will need to eliminate some policies and procedures, create a few new ones, and simply tweak others.

Some district leaders tend to develop policies or procedures for every possible contingency, regardless of how remote the possibility of its occurrence. It is more effective to have fewer policies related to those issues that will affect most of the people, most of the time. Of course, some things will arise that aren't covered by a specific policy, but it is much better to deal with those on a case-by-case basis than create dozens of policies and procedures that attempt to predict every possible situation. It is simply impossible to think of every possible contingency. Trying to create policies to cover anything that might occur, regardless of how remote the possibility, dilutes the importance of high-priority policies.

> *It is simply impossible to think of every possible contingency. Trying to create policies to cover anything that might occur, regardless of how remote the possibility, dilutes the importance of high-priority policies.*

Keep It Simple and Specific

As we discussed in chapter 2, words—and their meaning—matter. This is especially true in district policies and procedures. Vague and inconsistent language can cause confusion and create potential for legal challenges. When revising district policies and procedures, it is imperative that the language is consistent with state and federal laws and regulations, as well as the district's negotiated contract with the teachers' association. But most importantly, district leaders must make sure that policies and procedures communicate a clear, concise, and consistent message regarding the district's core purpose and the district's vision for the future. Clear and specific districtwide policies and procedures can go a long way to clarify communications and assist district leaders in speaking with one clear and concise voice.

Move From Hope to Certainty

Aligning policies, practices, and procedures is a critical strategy for moving a district culture from one of hope ("We hope everyone understands . . . ," "We hope faculty and staff will . . . ," and so on) to one of certainty—a culture in which the parameters of the work are communicated and clear to all. While this alignment cannot guarantee districtwide focus on student learning, the *absence* of alignment virtually guarantees that implementation of the learning mission will be disjointed and uneven throughout the district.

Clear, effective policies that are aligned with the core purpose of the district drive day-to-day practices. For example, if district leaders clearly and consistently communicate through their policies and procedures a strong commitment to ensuring high levels of student learning, appropriate practices in areas such as unit planning, student practice, the development and use of common formative assessments, grading, homework, student opportunity to redo work, and additional time, support, and enrichment will become increasingly obvious.

Monitor and Adjust

Often, there is a tendency to think that once district policies have been put in place, they become permanent. Nothing could be further from the truth! Simply because district leaders take time to critically analyze, adjust, and align district policies and procedures does not necessarily mean all of the decisions are correct. Policies and procedures must be seen as tools to promote the district's core purpose and vision, and from time to time, new tools will be needed and older tools discarded. Remember, if district leaders will simply view a school or even the district as "just a bigger classroom," they will follow the example of effective classroom teachers and constantly monitor and adjust.

One last word of caution is in order. Avoid the trap of thinking that once policies, practices, and procedures have been critically analyzed and aligned, you have completed the necessary work to ensure significant districtwide school improvement. Structure is never enough. If no attention is paid to the critical issues that shape school culture, your efforts will prove only marginally successful—if at all.

Reflections

While it is true that district leaders must pay attention to creating a *culture* supportive of ensuring high levels of learning for all students, leaders must also pay attention to the various *structures* within the district. Both culture and structure are important. They impact one another. One of the most important tasks leaders must undertake is aligning the district's policies, practices, and procedures with the district's learning mission and vision for the future.

Individually or in teams, reflect on questions such as the following.

1. Have leaders in your district made a conscientious effort to critically analyze and align district policies, practices, and procedures with a mission of ensuring high levels of student learning?

2. To what degree have agreed-upon policies, practices, and procedures been clearly communicated?

3. Are policies, practices, and procedures—such as the expectation that administrators, faculty, and staff must be contributing members of a collaborative team or teams—clearly communicated during the hiring process?

4. Do policies and procedures clearly articulate role expectations and responsibilities?

5. Are performance appraisal processes aligned with role responsibilities and expectations, the district's learning mission, and the district's vision for the future?

6. It is not unusual for district leaders to place heavy attention on policies but pay little attention to the daily procedures and practices that have a tremendous impact not only on district and school culture but on student achievement as well. To what degree have procedures and practices such as scheduling, homework, grading, and reporting pupil progress been analyzed and adjusted?

7. Are there any policies, practices, and procedures that you think should be addressed that have not been addressed?

8. Are there policies, practices, or procedures related directly to professional development that should be analyzed and improved on?

9. What processes do you think could be utilized to review and align your district (or school) policies, practices, and procedures?

10. What process does (or could) your district use to monitor and adjust policies, practices, and procedures on a regular basis?

Chapter 5

Leading Collaborative Teams

Most traditional schools promote a culture of teacher isolation—individual teachers are left on their own to teach. A professional learning community cultivates the exact opposite. Schools and districts that function as professional learning communities are driven by a *collaborative* culture in which teams work together to ensure all their students learn. DuFour, DuFour, Eaker, and Many (2010) describe the collaborative culture of a professional learning community by observing, "In a PLC, *collaboration* represents a systematic process in which teachers work together interdependently in order to *impact* their classroom practice in ways that will lead to better results for their students, for their team, and for their school" (p. 12).

The power of collaborative teams is old news. For at least a quarter of a century researchers and experts in organizational development have touted the efficacy of high-performing collaborative teams. Pfeffer and Sutton (2000) note, "Interdependence is what organizations are all about. Productivity, performance, and innovation result from *joint* action, not just individual efforts and behavior" (p. 197).

> *District leaders in a professional learning community embed a collaborative culture within the day-to-day life of each school by purposefully ensuring that teachers are organized into collaborative teams.*

For this reason, professional learning communities go beyond merely "inviting" or "encouraging" teachers to collaborate. District leaders in a professional learning community *embed* a collaborative culture within the day-to-day life of each school by purposefully ensuring that teachers are organized into collaborative teams, and they clearly and consistently communicate that the purpose of each team is to improve student learning. Most importantly, successful district leaders develop a collaborative culture with a sense of passion and commitment.

These leaders don't view organizing the district into collaborative teams as a technical add-on or something "we're going to kind of do." Rather, they envision collaborative teaming as *the* fundamental organizing structure of the district, *the way* the district operates every day, and no one is allowed to opt out! District leaders must understand that improving student learning will depend on the effectiveness of each individual team, and they must accept the responsibility of ensuring that each team performs at a high level of quality. In short, collaborative teams must be seen by district leaders as the power source, the heart and soul, of a district that seeks to function as a professional learning community.

Define the Work

Professional learning communities go beyond merely organizing the faculty and staff into teams. Leaders of professional learning communities are crystal clear about what the work of collaborative teams should be and what products teams will be asked to produce. For example, teacher teams will be expected to:

- Clarify the essential outcomes for each subject or course
- Collaboratively develop common daily learning targets for each standard
- Develop common formative assessments, and collaboratively analyze and utilize the results
- Monitor the learning of each student on a frequent and timely basis, skill by skill
- Participate in the development of systematic plans to provide students with additional time, support, and enrichment
- Reflect on and share with other team members their own instructional practices in order to improve their individual effectiveness, as well as the team's effectiveness
- Engage in collective inquiry

We aren't suggesting that traditional schools don't collaborate at all. They collaborate in any number of ways. However, one of the major differences between the collaborative culture of traditional schools versus collaborative teaming in a professional learning community centers on the processes for making decisions. Teachers in traditional schools collaborate largely by averaging opinions. During meetings, everyone has the opportunity to share his or her opinions and make suggestions. Each opinion is treated as though it has equal value, and ownership of a recommendation often trumps the efficacy of what is being proposed—that is, it's more important that teachers *agree* on a decision than make the *best* decision.

Professional learning communities operate from a different set of assumptions. Collaborative teams in a professional learning community always approach a problem or issue by first building shared knowledge—studying the *best that is known* about the particular topic being addressed—and making decisions based on what will be best for student learning.

In this respect, collaborative teams in a professional learning community are merely mirroring the behavior of other professionals. For example, when a patient is treated by a physician, the patient has every right to expect that what the physician does is based on the best knowledge available at that time. In all professions, the knowledge base is constantly changing and improving as more becomes known. It is a professional's responsibility to constantly seek new knowledge regarding the latest and most effective practices, and then to incorporate the behaviors into his or her daily practice. Constantly seeking and practicing best practice is an essential characteristic of a professional learning community.

A word of caution is in order. Seeking best practice doesn't necessarily mean teams always have to look to formal research for answers. Since professional learning communities are ultimately a culture of experimentation, best practice is often found within the team itself. Best practice may be found on other teams in the same school, at another school in the district, or at a school in a neighboring district. Additionally, books, articles, professional development meetings, professional organizations, and the Internet are all valuable resources. The point is this: collaborative teams in a school or district that functions as a professional learning community become *students of best practice*.

Build Shared Knowledge

Successful districts model PLC practices by making sure the faculty and staff gain a clear understanding of the power of collaborative teams, why the district is organizing into teams, and most important, what the collaborative teams will be expected to do.

This step is critical because most faculty and staff have preconceived ideas about collaboration. Some think collaboration is simply discussing issues or problems, sharing ideas, or participating in a book study. Many equate collaboration with collegiality, and some display the attitude that "We are already a team, we've been teaming forever!" It is not uncommon for faculty and staff to remark that they already collaborate, that they're nice, that they serve on committees together, and that they talk to one another over lunch or at school events.

There are two inherent problems with this view of collaboration. First, it is limited; it lacks intention, the specific purpose of improving student learning. Secondly, it doesn't include *everyone*. It's only natural that people who like each other find it more pleasant to collaborate and share, while people who are not so well liked might be left out. However, if the core purpose of the collaboration is clear, and the purpose is to improve learning in specific content areas, teams have a reason for including everyone, regardless of likeability.

In White River, we wanted to be absolutely clear about what teams in a professional learning community do. There is a tendency for teams to fall back on what they know—talking about student behavior or the latest school and district rumors, and so on. In clarifying what collaborative teams are and what they do, we always refer districts to the definitions that appear in *Learning by Doing* (DuFour, DuFour, Eaker, & Many, 2010). We clearly and consistently communicated this message: "Collaborative teams are characterized by team members working interdependently to achieve common goals, for which they will hold themselves mutually accountable." Additionally, we provided training that included videos of collaborative teams actually doing the work of a professional learning community.

Simply organizing into collaborative teams will have little, if any, impact on student learning. The critical issue that must be addressed is what the teams are expected to do. Therefore, it is essential that district and building leaders develop various approaches to guide and monitor the work of collaborative teams. The planning form in figure 5.1 is used in the White River School District to help teams understand that district leaders are tight about the work that is to be done, but loose as to when the work will be done within a set time frame. For example, at the top of the monthly planning form is a list of the focus of the work for that particular month. These directions come from the district office in collaboration with the team of principals. However, *when* the work will be done within each month is left to the discretion of each team or school.

In short, we urge district leaders to make sure everyone has a clear understanding of what the term *collaborative team* means, what successful teams do, and how collaborative teams in a professional learning community differ from more traditional notions of faculty and staff collaboration. The goal is simply to remove the mystery surrounding what this teaming will look on a day-to-day basis within the district. See page 178 in the appendix for a sample districtwide email on this topic: "Collaborative Teams in a Professional Learning Community."

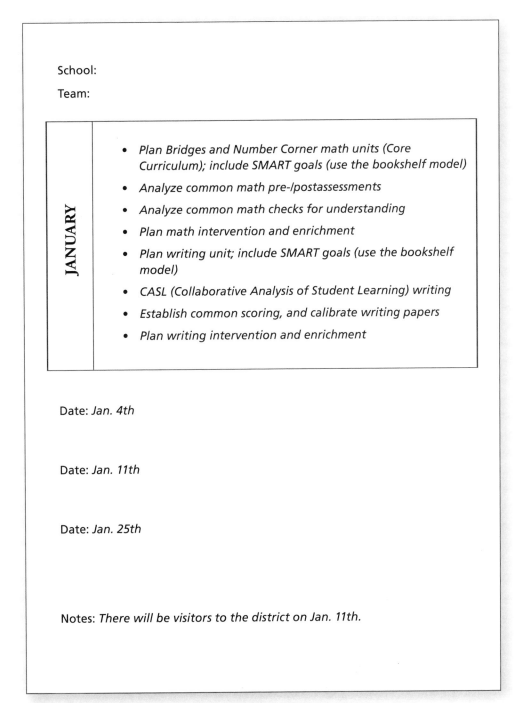

School:

Team:

JANUARY	<ul><li>*Plan Bridges and Number Corner math units (Core Curriculum); include SMART goals (use the bookshelf model)*</li><li>*Analyze common math pre-/postassessments*</li><li>*Analyze common math checks for understanding*</li><li>*Plan math intervention and enrichment*</li><li>*Plan writing unit; include SMART goals (use the bookshelf model)*</li><li>*CASL (Collaborative Analysis of Student Learning) writing*</li><li>*Establish common scoring, and calibrate writing papers*</li><li>*Plan writing intervention and enrichment*</li></ul>

Date: *Jan. 4th*

Date: *Jan. 11th*

Date: *Jan. 25th*

Notes: *There will be visitors to the district on Jan. 11th.*

Figure 5.1: Sample team planning guide.

Source: White River School District. Used with permission.

Begin With the Principals

It is common practice in more traditional district cultures for principals simply to inform faculty and staff of a new initiative or direct them to do it. Our experience has been that the quality of the work of *teacher teams* is directly tied to the quality of the work of the *principal team*. In other words, before asking teachers to be contributing members of a collaborative team, district leaders—and especially the principals—must first learn to function as a successful team that focuses on the right things.

> *The quality of the work of* teacher teams *is directly tied to the quality of the work of the* principal team.

As we noted in chapter 1, one of the most important steps is to organize the principals into a collaborative team or teams, depending on the size of the district. (The district office must also organize into teams, serving as a model for the other teams within the district.) Principals who serve on collaborative teams themselves are able to anticipate questions and issues that might arise when teacher teams are engaged in the work of improving student learning, and are able to *practice and rehearse*, as a team, what they will ultimately expect of teacher teams. Most important, the principal teams are expected to share student learning data and to share and learn best practice from each other in exactly the same way teacher teams will be expected to perform. In short, effective districts are dedicated to the notion that the principal team must model the behavior expected of others—and work out the kinks *before* embedding the new practice in schools.

Figure 5.2 summarizes the process of creating a high-performing collaborative culture. It begins with district-level teaming, where principals (and other district leaders) anticipate issues and questions, practice and rehearse the work that will be expected of teacher teams, and share learning data. Principals then engage in the same processes with their team leaders in regularly scheduled team meetings. Only after principals and team leaders have anticipated issues and concerns, practiced and rehearsed the work that will be expected of collaborative teams, and shared and analyzed student learning data, do collaborative teacher teams engage in the same practices and processes. District leaders who are committed to improving the quality of work of teacher teams start by improving the quality of work expected of districtwide principal teams.

Embed Collaborative Teams Districtwide

Again, in the most successful districts with which we have worked, district leaders did not "invite" or "provide the opportunity" for teachers to work in

District-Level Principal Teams

- Are composed of principals from throughout the district
- Develop role definitions and shared commitments
- Develop and adhere to team norms
- Focus on learning
- Hold regular meetings, with agendas, for decision making
- Anticipate issues and questions
- Practice and rehearse the work
- Share learning data
- Seek best practice, share, practice, and plan
- Monitor results; seek continuous improvement
- Model behavior expected of others

School-Level Team Leader Teams

- Are composed of principal, assistant principals, and team leaders
- Develop role definitions and shared commitments
- Develop and adhere to team norms
- Focus on learning
- Hold regular meetings, with agendas, for decision making
- Anticipate issues and questions
- Practice and rehearse the work
- Share learning data
- Analyze student learning, seek best practice, share, practice, and plan
- Monitor results; seek continuous improvement
- Model behavior expected of others

Collaborative Teacher Teams

- Are composed of teachers who teach the same content
- Develop and adhere to team norms
- Focus on learning
- Hold regular meetings, with agendas, for decision making
- Anticipate issues and questions
- Practice and rehearse the work
- Share learning data
- Analyze student learning, seek best practice, share, practice, and plan
- Monitor results; seek continuous improvement

Figure 5.2: Collaborative team responsibilities and development.

collaborative teams. Instead, they made it clear that collaborative teams would be the basic organizing structure across the district.

Team structures can vary by school level and size, as long as team members teach common content. For example, an elementary teacher would be on the second-grade team or the fifth-grade team, depending on the grade level she taught. In a small school, teachers might be organized into a vertical team spanning prekindergarten to second grade instead. A middle or high school teacher might be a member of the math team; in larger schools, a math teacher might serve on two teams, spending the majority of his or her time with a course-specific team—for example, an algebra team or a geometry team. (*Learning by Doing* [DuFour, DuFour, Eaker, & Many, 2010] is an excellent resource on options for organizing teacher teams.)

While there can be great latitude in how the teams are organized, set a specific date set by which the entire district is to be organized into collaborative teams. Again, the leadership skills of principals and their experience working in teams prior to districtwide implementation are key; teachers will have questions and concerns, of course, and principals must be prepared to answer questions, give clear directions, provide examples, and quickly clarify misunderstandings.

In White River, we wanted to create a culture in which teachers never even realized there was such a thing as working in isolation. Think of it: new teachers who have been working in White River five years or less have never experienced working in isolation. It's only natural that first-year teachers feel particularly overwhelmed. Being placed on a truly high-performing team in a school and district that functions as a professional learning community is the best thing that can ever happen to a new teacher. Time and again we have seen new teachers who at the end of their first year perform on par with their veteran colleagues because they enjoyed the support of a collaborative team.

Select Team Leaders Carefully

Just as district success depends on the leadership capability of superintendents, and school success depends on the leadership behavior of principals, the success of collaborative teams depends on the leadership capacity of team leaders.

In White River, we also realized that the quality of work performed by teams would depend, to a great degree, on team leaders joining with their principal to direct the work of the teams and ensure that teams were focusing on the right things. Just as district success depends on the leadership capability of superintendents, and school success depends on the leadership behavior of principals, the success of collaborative teams depends on the leadership capacity of team leaders. After all, there is a reason they are referred to as team *leaders*.

Ironically, the role of team leader is one of the least examined aspects of school structure and culture. Think about how team leaders are selected in more traditional schools: the "strategies" range from asking for volunteers, to seniority, to deal making ("We're willing to let you, if you are willing to do it"), to automatically rotating to a new leader each year, to voting, to using the role of team leader to provide leadership opportunities for all teachers. One team with which we are familiar shared with us that it used the "huddle up" strategy. It went like this: "You have ten minutes to huddle up with your department and pick your team leader!" In short, in many districts, the role of team leader—what the leader is to do and how he or she is selected—is a thoughtless process.

Compare this to how team leaders are selected in other aspects of schooling. For example, think about how the head football coach at the high school selects his coaching staff. He gives considerable thought to who should fill each role. He doesn't just rotate his offensive coordinator each year or search for volunteers! Instead, he thoughtfully selects the best person to fill the position, the position is well defined, and the role expectations are clearly communicated.

At White River, our first step in addressing the role of team leader was to collaboratively develop a position description. We realized it was simply unreasonable to have expectations of team leaders without providing clarity about what the role entailed. While each school culture in the district was different, we expected a few things would be consistent in each school. For example, team leaders would be expected to lead the team in tasks such as:

- Developing and adhering to team norms
- Clarifying and adding meaning to essential learning outcomes for each subject or course
- Developing and utilizing common formative assessments
- Analyzing student learning student by student, skill by skill
- Directing students to specific additional time and support or enrichment
- Seeking out and sharing best practice
- Collaboratively planning units
- Developing and monitoring the attainment of SMART goals

Collaboratively developed position descriptions can clarify the role of the team leader. However, a word of caution is in order; if written or interpreted too narrowly, position descriptions can prove to be not only ineffective but a problem. We have found it useful to include sample responsibilities, activities, and tasks, rather than definitive lists. Figure 5.3 shows the position description we created at White River.

Additionally, we gave considerable attention to the relationship between the principal and team leaders. Emphasizing the role of the team leader is another way White River implemented layered leadership. Clarifying roles and relationships helped us communicate that the purpose of the position description was to make the work more transparent. We wanted faculty and staff to understand they still had access to the principal; principals were not shielding themselves from the teacher teams by emphasizing the importance of team leaders. We also expected team leaders to keep a notebook containing the various products the team had developed, such as team norms, power standards, and common assessments. Team leaders brought their notebooks to each team leader meeting with the principal.

Just as principals should be part of a high-performing administrative team at the district level, team leaders should play an integral role as members of principals' leadership team at the school level. Leaders of professional learning communities—whether at the district, school, or team level—are constantly and consistently modeling the work of high-performing collaborative teams. That is, they focus on improving student learning and developing a culture of continuous improvement; they practice and rehearse the work that ultimately will be expected of others.

District and building leaders must also give considerable thought to the kind of training and support team leaders need in order to be successful. It is impossible for team leaders to perform their duties at a high level unless they are provided with support, resources, and training. One approach we utilized at White River involved district leaders and principals developing various scenarios that reflected realistic, difficult issues teams were likely to encounter. These role-playing exercises provided examples that were not only educational but nonthreatening. Most important, they helped teams anticipate and respond to issues and questions they would likely face in the future.

Plan for the "Singletons"

One of the most frequently asked questions we hear centers on faculty or staff who are the only ones teaching a particular subject or course, or the only ones in the school fulfilling unique roles, such as librarian, music teacher, and many career and technical education teachers. Districts and schools across North America have successfully implemented strategies for providing a collaborative culture for singletons. However, developing these plans requires flexibility, creativity, and district-level support.

A high-performing collaborative team of teachers is the heart and soul of a school that functions as a professional learning community, and a highly effective team is invariably led by an effective team leader. The success of the White River School District to achieve its mission of ensuring high levels of learning for all students depends to a great degree on the leadership capacity of the team leaders in each school. Thus, the selection of team leaders in White River is a thoughtful, informed, and deliberate decision of critical importance.

The educators who serve in this very important role are expected to coordinate and lead the work of their team. They will work closely with the Learning Improvement Coordinator within their building and report directly to the building principal. Additionally, team leaders serve as a contributing member of the principal's administrative team. Team leaders are expected to articulate and communicate faculty questions, needs, and concerns to the administration, as well as to communicate and explain the rationale and specifics of the administration's plans and initiatives to the faculty. In short, the team leader serves as the key communications link between the administration and the faculty.

Team leaders are expected to enhance the capacity of their team to work interdependently to achieve common goals for which team members hold themselves mutually accountable. In fulfilling this role, the team leader is responsible for such functions as leading the team in preparing and utilizing team norms, planning agendas, chairing meetings, serving as a direct communications link between the administration and the faculty, leading the work of teams in analyzing and improving student learning data, seeking out and experimenting with best practices, leading the collaborative development and attainment of learning improvement goals, and identifying and communicating professional development needs. Team leaders must work to continually enhance the effectiveness of their team by ensuring that the team focuses on the critical questions and practices associated with improving student learning in a manner that is reflective of the highest quality.

Educators who serve as team leaders must have a demonstrated record of effectiveness in their own teaching, and they must have earned the recognition and respect of their peers. Team leaders must have excellent planning and organizational skills, as well as the ability to work well with others. In order to enhance the leadership capacity and effectiveness of others, team leaders must model a desire and willingness to continually learn—they must be constantly seeking ways to first improve themselves so that they can more effectively lead their team.

In short, the White River School District is seeking outstanding individuals to lead building-level collaborative teams of teachers in order to more effectively impact student learning levels—student by student, skill by skill, relentlessly and continually!

Figure 5.3: Position description for team leader.

Source: White River School District. Used with permission.

In White River, as well as in other districts with which we've worked, we scheduled regular times when, for example, librarians, music teachers, advanced placement teachers, or special education teachers from across the district could meet together. Sometimes the singletons worked as contributing members of electronic teams. At other times they met with other teams in the school in order to provide specific assistance or information.

There is only one rule that applied to the singletons: they must collaborate with colleagues in meaningful ways, and they must focus on the critical issues related to student learning. To learn more about how other districts dealt with this issue, turn to *Learning by Doing* (DuFour, DuFour, Eaker, & Many, 2010), which contains very specific suggestions, and or visit www.allthingsplc.info to find blog entries on this topic and an extensive list of schools that can be contacted for suggestions.

We like to remind the districts with which we work that faculty and staff are only singletons if they choose to be—*and if they are allowed to be*! In White River, we simply asked, "Would you want your own child educated by someone who hasn't engaged in deep, professional collaboration with other teachers about content-specific work for twenty years?"

Provide Time for Team Collaboration

Collaborative teams need a number of resources to be successful, but the most basic resource they require is time—time to work collaboratively together to improve student learning. To be effective, the district must provide teacher teams time to do their work within the school day. Don't ask them to carry the PLC work home with them in their backpacks so they can work on it at night, or before school each morning. That simply will not work. Teams need a minimum of one hour per week of collaborative team time built into the school schedule.

Districts and schools across North America have found creative ways to solve the time problem. There is absolutely no reason why other districts cannot do the same. District leaders should not depend on principals figuring out creative ways to find time, even with encouragement; finding time for teams to meet usually requires district leadership and support.

Start by learning how other schools and districts have tackled the time problem, then find time where you can, bit by bit, always with the goal of finding new and incremental ways of providing teams with the time they need to do their work—within the school day. First look at how existing meeting time is being utilized. As noted in chapter 4, shift the focus from informational topics that can be communicated electronically or in other formats to the more significant issues related to improving student learning.

Many districts use either late starts or early-release days to create regular collaborative team planning time. In White River, we found the late start to be more effective than an early release for a variety of reasons, the most basic being that everyone, including coaches, is available in the morning. So, after demonstrating the impact collaborative teaming can have on student learning, the White River school board approved a one-hour late start each Monday morning so that teams would have regularly scheduled meeting time within the school day across the district.

We knew this particular approach would only be effective if (and this is a huge "if") the purpose and benefits of the planning time were thoroughly and consistently communicated to parents and the larger community, and the focus of the teams' work was clearly articulated and monitored. Thoughtful, carefully planned public relations are critical to the success of changes in scheduling. Parents always have a number of questions related to what teachers will be doing during the collaborative time, and responses to parent inquiries must be accurate, consistent, and helpful. In White River, we armed every person who answered the phone with the same seven-second response describing what teacher teams would be doing during the late starts and how it would benefit the learning of each child.

Some families have unique circumstances that require flexibility and creativity from district leaders. We developed a number of alternatives for students who simply had no choice but to arrive at the regularly scheduled times, alternatives such as art classes, science classes, library time, and district childcare options. It is impossible to anticipate each and every possible situation, so an attitude of "We'll figure this out and make it work for you" is essential.

Get Organized, and Get Started

One of the most significant things we have learned from White River is that the quality of work is directly related to how well the district plans and organizes the activities and tasks are to be performed.

Doing high-quality work requires districtwide organization and planning, which in turn instills a sense of confidence in the faculty and staff. Simple things, such as providing binders for each principal and each team, send the message that we expect teams to be organized in their work. At White River, the binders were delivered to each school preloaded with examples of the work of high-performing collaborative teams. For example, the first tab held examples of norms. The next tab included sample power standards, the next tab examples of a pacing guide, the next examples of common assessments, and so on. As teams did their work, they added their products to their binder. Additionally, much of the work was electronically stored for access by the district office. We wanted, for example, for a first-year teacher to be able to click into ninth-grade algebra and be able to find the ninth-grade algebra power standards for first and second semester, along with the pacing guide and common assessments. A third-grade teacher could click into the writing curriculum and see the power standards, evidence of learning rubrics for each standard, and common scoring guides.

The teams also complete a very basic weekly feedback form that is emailed to the principal after the team meeting. This form highlights the work that was accomplished that week at the team meeting and only takes a few minutes to complete. The most important section on the form is the portion titled "Building Administrator's Needs." If a team is struggling, needs specific resources, or needs the help of another team or help from staff in the district office, we want the principal to know immediately. We don't want teams to become frustrated, or the principal to find out six weeks too late that they needed assistance.

Monitor and Improve the Work of Teams

Just as teacher teams are expected to monitor learning student by student, skill by skill, principals are expected to monitor effectiveness team by team, task by task.

These tools not only aid teams in doing their work, they aid leaders in monitoring and improving the work of teams. As noted earlier, just as effective classroom teachers monitor the learning of each student in a frequent and timely manner, we expect principals to accept the responsibility for the effectiveness of *each* team within their school. Just as teacher teams are expected to monitor learning student by student, skill by skill, principals are expected to monitor effectiveness team by team, task by task.

Teams will respond to differing leadership styles and approaches, and will also do the work associated with a focus on learning at differing rates. Leaders cannot assume the work is, in fact, being done by every team. Effective leaders do more than simply have a "feel" for where each team is and the work members are doing. They monitor the performance of each team, making sure it is doing the right work, at a high level of quality.

It is important to review the products of teams with team leaders for that reason. For example, at White River, we expected our teams to constantly tweak their common assessments, making them better. We expected that their assessment questions were aligned with the standards and learning targets, and that the questions were crafted in a way to accurately collect the information we were looking for. We expected teams to pay attention to the taxonomy of learning when developing common assessment questions. We knew that sometimes we would need to rewrite an assessment question. At times the state standards would change, and we would need to adjust our power standards. We needed to create and support a culture of tweaking. At White River, the team binders greatly facilitated product review, and at the bottom of virtually every document in White River are the revision dates.

Principals in White River used other tools to monitor team effectiveness, too. The form in figure 5.4 (page 102) was used to make sure that each team was focusing on the right work at the right time. Tasks listed in the left column result in the products team leaders include in their team leader notebooks. Note the inclusion of celebration planning and target dates for completion of each step. Principals and team leaders then used the form in figure 5.5 (page 103) to provide feedback on the quality of the team's work by summarizing its strengths and identifying areas for improvement. Finally, teams self-monitored by using the more detailed "Critical Issues for Team Consideration" that is found in *Learning by Doing* (DuFour, DuFour, Eaker, & Many, 2010, pp. 130–131).

However, just as simply monitoring learning levels will do little to improve student learning, monitoring the work of teams must result in action to be effective. The fact is, it's the *quality* of interventions, both for students and adults, that ultimately matters. We urge districts to collaboratively develop pyramids of interventions for teams that are experiencing difficulty, just as we do for struggling students. Just as Tier 1 interventions for students primarily take place within the classroom, Tier 1 interventions for teams should be accomplished within the team. For example, teams may need to revisit, revise, or merely recommit to their norms. We recommend the self-assessment instruments and strategies for next steps in *Learning by Doing* (DuFour, DuFour, Eaker, & Many, 2010). The team leader may seek advice from the principal or others or merely engage in deep, meaningful, direct conversations with either the entire team or with individual team members.

However, what if these efforts produce only meager results? Again, interventions for improving team effectiveness should mirror the approach that is taken for improving student learning when Tier 1 interventions fail. That is, we move to Tier 2 interventions, which are more focused and rely on resources beyond the team itself. For example, the principal, working with the team leader, might arrange for training or additional resources such as articles, books, or videos, or perhaps a consultant. The team leader may present the problem to the School Leadership Team and ask fellow team leaders for advice. Perhaps the principal will be asked to observe a few team meetings and provide feedback and advice. Some school districts assist principals in arranging visits to observe high-performing teams, either within the district or within neighboring districts.

Task	Team 1	Target Date	Team 2	Target Date	Team 3	Target Date	Team 4	Target Date
Develop team norms.								
Identify power standards and develop common pacing guides.								
Create written meeting agendas.								
Write common assessments.								
Analyze the results of common assessments.								
Develop a systematic plan for time, support, and enrichment.								
Develop a plan to celebrate improvement of students.								
Develop a plan to celebrate improvement of adults.								
Analyze student work.								

Figure 5.4: Teamwork monitoring form.

Source: White River School District. Used with permission.

Visit **go.solution-tree.com/plcbooks** to download a reproducible version of this figure.

What Effective Teams Do

- Develop and use team norms.
- Clarify and add meaning to state or provincial standards and district power standards.
- Clarify what standards look like in student work.
- Develop and utilize common pacing guides.
- Develop common formative assessments.
- Develop common scoring rubrics.

- Monitor results by collaboratively analyzing student learning (work and assessments).
- Connect student learning to appropriate interventions or enrichment.
- Work collaboratively to improve their individual instructional practices.
- Work collaboratively to improve team effectiveness.
- Improve student learning.

School: _____ Team: _____

Narrative Analysis of Team Effectiveness

_____
_____
_____
_____

Team Next Steps for School Year _____

_____
_____
_____
_____

Support That Will Be Provided to the Team

_____
_____
_____
_____

Figure 5.5: Team effectiveness monitoring form for principals and team leaders.

Source: White River School District. Used with permission.

If interventions from both Tier 1 and Tier 2 fail, the team will need much more direct and radical help: Tier 3 interventions. Perhaps the principal will meet with the team regularly and direct that certain things occur. Perhaps the principal will need to name a new team leader or reconfigure the makeup of the team. In White River, principals were expected to take ownership for the effectiveness of each team within their school and, in a systematic, timely, and direct way, ensure and enhance the effectiveness of each team.

Figure 5.6 depicts examples of the kinds of interventions that can be useful in enhancing team effectiveness. We have found the pyramid to be useful for district leaders to engage principals and team leaders in a collaborative process that leads to the development of their own plan for providing additional time and support for teams that experience difficulty.

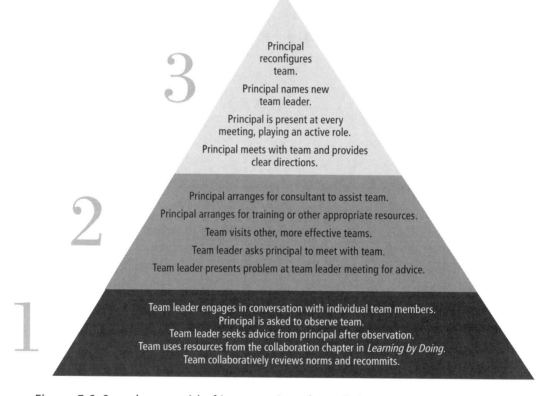

Figure 5.6: Sample pyramid of interventions for collaborative teams.

Source: White River School District. Used with permission.

What We Have Learned About Leading Collaborative Teams

As we mentioned earlier, collaborative teams are the heart and soul of a district seeking to improve student achievement. Our work with numerous districts that have utilized collaborative teams as the fundamental organizing structure throughout the district have led to a number of insights.

Again, Get Started, Then Get Better

Many district leaders become bogged down waiting until every issue is resolved before embedding the use of collaborative teams in each school. The most successful districts are crystal clear in their expectation that each principal must utilize collaborative teams as the primary organizational structure of their school. District leaders must *lead* the effort to make sure that principals and, initially, a small guiding coalition gain a deep, rich understanding of how effective teams work and what effective teams do. But, most important, district leaders must *insist* that collaborative teams focus on the right things discussed in this chapter.

How well collaborative teams perform depends to an extraordinary degree on the *quality* of the structural work that has been done previously (and described earlier in this book). Much of this foundational work is not glamorous, but time and attention put into developing these foundational pieces will pay huge dividends later.

Insist That Everyone Collaborates

Despite our best efforts, some team members may just go through the motions. A teacher can do the work of a team while at the team meeting, but go back to the classroom and do whatever he or she wants. Some teachers are happy working in isolation. They like the content they're teaching and the way they are teaching, regardless of how well their students learned. The question of whether the kids are actually learning isn't their main concern. They are more interested in *teaching* content that is of interest to *them*. Some will even be so blunt as to say, "I don't need to look at data. I can tell you what the data say without looking at them." One can only hope that other professionals on whom we depend, such as doctors, dentists, accountants, and attorneys, do not view data with similar disdain.

> *In every district with which we have worked, we have urged district leaders to make doing the right work, in the right way, at the right time, and in collaboration with colleagues, non-negotiable.*

Analyzing the results of common assessments will really flesh a few of those people out. It becomes obvious when they come to the table that they don't have their common assessment data, that they weren't teaching what they needed to be teaching, or that they weren't using the assessments that they needed to use to measure student learning. In essence, they have nothing to share. This leads to difficult, but necessary, conversations. In every district with which we have worked, we have urged district leaders to make doing the right work, in the right way, at the right time, and in collaboration with colleagues, non-negotiable.

Connect Principal Teams and Teacher Teams

While many factors affect the effectiveness of teacher teams within individual schools, a critical factor that is often overlooked is the connection between the quality of the work of the districtwide principal team and teacher teams. Again, principals must practice, in districtwide principal team meetings, the behaviors that will be expected of teacher teams in each building. When principals at the district-level principal team meetings have engaged in and practiced the work that is expected of the teacher teams back in their schools, they are in a much better position to assist teacher teams in doing the complex work of improving student learning. This is one of the most difficult, yet important, aspects of creating a districtwide collaborative culture that utilizes the power of collaborative teams.

In many districts, principals attend meetings at the district level, then simply pass the information on to teachers—never actually engaging in the work themselves. They are much like matadors, simply waving a cape to let information from the district office charge past. Imagine a principal taking notes at a district meeting, then reporting to the faculty, "Last week I was told that *they* want *you* to . . ." This communicates that the principal has no personal stake in the work and is merely the messenger!

It's true that principals often find themselves in the position of facing questions that they may not be capable of adequately answering. So practice is important to gain knowledge. For example, when it was time to analyze the results of our common assessments at White River, the principals' team practiced analyzing the results of common assessments first. The principals anticipated the questions that might arise from teams and worked out any issues that surfaced *before* they asked their teacher teams to analyze the results of common assessments. When principals possess the knowledge and skills they expect of others, their credibility and effectiveness are enhanced tremendously.

Use Formative Assessment and Differentiated Leadership

Our work with numerous districts has taught us that team learning reflects what takes place in student learning—some people get it immediately, and some struggle and need help. We cannot assume because every member of the faculty and staff heard the same message, read the same material, or even attended the same training sessions, that they all have the same degree of understanding, competence, or even commitment. This is where the persistence of district and building leaders, and their ability to provide differentiated leadership, becomes critical (see fig. 5.7).

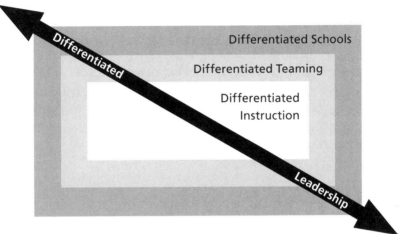

Figure 5.7: The differentiated leadership model.

Formative assessment and differentiated instruction aren't just for the classroom. Principals must develop systems and processes to monitor the work of collaborative teams within their buildings on a frequent and timely basis and, as with students, differentiate their responses based on the needs of each individual team—constantly working to enhance the effectiveness of every team. Effective principals organize the work in very specific and detailed ways, listen to conversations, provide teams with high-quality examples of products that teams will be asked to develop, examine the products the teams create, and then determine next steps for that team.

Provide Examples and Visuals

If we want teams to be able to do the work, we have to provide them with clear examples of what we are looking for. We don't want the team sitting at the table saying, "I wonder what this is supposed to look like? I'm not sure what the principal wants us to do." When the teams have clear examples of our expectations, the work goes much smoother. Examples can accelerate the work, and excellent examples can serve as a standard of quality. Importantly, examples can also send the message, "They did it, so can you!" Faculty and staff often think the work is more complex and complicated than it is in reality. Examples can let everyone "see" what products resulting from the work looks like. Leaders in the White River School District used examples from within the district and from other districts at every stage of their journey to becoming a professional learning community. Visit **go.solution-tree.com/plcbooks** to access examples of essential outcomes, common formative assessments, and plans for intervention and enrichment.

So provide examples, but be sure teams know they are also expected to put their own stamp on their products. The work must be useful for them—not merely an activity to create something to turn in. Teams need to clearly see that the purpose of the work is to improve student learning.

Visuals that help teams understand the big picture of a professional learning community and where each task fits under each of the four critical questions are also important. The four critical questions are not separate initiatives, and teams need to see that all the work they do fits under one of the four questions.

For example, think about the first question: What do we want our kids to learn? We wanted the teams to see the work of identifying the power standards/ essential outcomes, surfacing daily learning targets, and creating a pacing guide, all fits under that first question. We also linked the work surrounding question one to the research and work of Bob Marzano; that is, developing a guaranteed and viable curriculum.

As teams worked on the second question (How do we know that they've learned it?), we explicitly let teams know this is where we would build shared knowledge surrounding assessment literacy, write common assessments, develop common daily checks for understanding, and analyze the assessment results. In the absence of a visual, teams just see the work as one more thing that the district offices are asking them to do, versus this is *their* work and they're moving through the scope of their work with the goal of ensuring more kids are learning more.

Publically Share the Work

When teams create products such as essential outcomes or common assessments, make the work public. This is an important way teams learn from one another. For example, at White River, when one team shared its first common assessment with a larger group, it quickly realized it had not paid attention to the taxonomy of learning. The team members had crafted all their questions at the information level only. They were quick to go back and make the necessary adjustments, making the assessment better.

Focus on Results

Time and time again we have witnessed districts commit to the *idea* of embedding collaborative teaming throughout the district, and even commit to teams doing the right work. Yet frequently district leaders fail to take the critical step of making sure principals understand that ensuring the effectiveness of *each* team within their school is their responsibility, for which they will be held accountable.

This question of accountability raises fundamental questions about assessing team effectiveness. While assessing the quality of team products, such as team norms and common assessments, can provide district leaders with useful insights, the ultimate measure of team effectiveness is *results*: are all students learning at higher levels, and how do we know? Look for evidence of student learning rather than of how well folks got along. Constantly ask, "Is the work of the collaborative team improving professional practice? Are more kids learning more as a result of the work of the team?"

Celebrate, Celebrate, Celebrate

Again, remember that students aren't the only ones who are motivated by recognition and celebration. We must celebrate at each stage in the journey—every time significant work is successfully completed.

> *Constantly recognize and publically celebrate the work as it is being done—at each step along the way.*

Let's face it; adults quickly figure out what is truly valued by what is publically and frequently celebrated. Therefore, if we proclaim that collaborative teams should engage in work designed to focus on and improve student learning, then we must recognize and publically celebrate teams exhibiting exemplary work.

Don't wait until the work is completely finished to recognize and celebrate the hard work of individuals and groups. (Remember, the work is never actually *finished*.) Rather, constantly recognize and publically celebrate the work as it is being done—at each step along the way. The fact is, doing the work associated with embedding a deep, rich focus on the learning of individual students, skill by skill, is difficult and complex, and it is important that faculty and staff know their work is being recognized and appreciated. These celebrations need not be elaborate; they must only be sincere, frequent, and associated directly with the *quality* of work that is expected.

Reflections

The word *community* in the phrase *professional learning community* is of critical importance, since the mission of improving learning levels of all students cannot be achieved as long as teachers work in isolation. Collaborative teaming is the engine that drives a professional learning community.

Individually or in teams, reflect on questions such as the following.

1. After reading this chapter, realistically, what is the current reality of teaming in your district or school? How do you know?

2. Is there an assessment process to determine the effectiveness of each individual collaborative team in each school in your district? If not, is there a process in your school?

3. To what degree have teams in your district or school focused on the right work of collaborative teams in a professional learning community? Are there teams that still have not accomplished specific tasks such as writing and utilizing team norms or collaboratively identifying and clarifying the essential outcomes in each subject, grade, or course?

4. Have principals in your district fully embraced the idea that it is the principal's responsibility to enhance the effectiveness of each team in their school?

5. At the district level, does the principal team collaboratively anticipate questions and issues that are likely to arise, practice and rehearse the work that ultimately will be expected of collaborative teams of teachers, and share learning data?

6. Is there a system in place in your district or school to monitor student learning team by team, student by student, essential skill by skill?

7. Have collaborative teams been engaged in appropriate training, and have teams received the additional resources they need in order to be successful?

8. How has the work of collaborative teams been publically recognized and celebrated within your district or school?

Chapter 6

Ensuring a Focus on Student Learning

When young students return home from school, parents often greet them by asking, "So, what did you learn today?" They don't ask, "So, what were you taught today?" The fact is, most parents—and educators—know there is a tremendous difference between what students are *taught* and what they actually *learn*. A focus on learning is the organizing principle of districts, schools, and teams—and classrooms—that function as true professional learning communities. All of the previous work we have described to this point, both structurally and culturally, was for the purpose of laying the foundation for an intense, passionate, and relentless focus on the learning of every single student within the district.

This cultural shift is often greeted with what appears to be widespread agreement. No one raises a hand to comment, "Well, I just can't agree with the notion that we should focus on the learning of our students!" The problem is that while many educators agree that student learning is obviously desirable, at a deeper level they either do not believe it strongly enough to do the things necessary to ensure that all students learn at high levels or they do not know how do so. But if a district publically declares ensuring high levels of student learning for all students as its core purpose, and *really means it*, educators within the district will act in fundamentally different ways. They will engage in a sharp and persistent focus on the critical questions associated with learning, and they will do this work in collaborative teams.

For example, *if we really mean it* when we say we are going to focus passionately and persistently on the learning of each student, rather than leaving it up to individual teachers to determine the meaning of standards and their relative importance, collaborative teams would clarify and determine the meaning of the standards in each subject, grade, and course, determine the relative importance of each standard, and develop common pacing guides. Rather than incrementally adding more and more to the curriculum, teacher teams would eliminate extraneous content from the curriculum, constantly seek ways to teach less but more significant content, at greater depth and in more meaningful ways.

And *if we really mean it* when we declare a mission of ensuring high levels of learning for all students, rather than relying almost solely on summative assessments to determine if students have learned, teams of teachers would develop common formative assessments designed to monitor learning on a frequent and timely basis, constantly seeking, student by student, skill by skill, to answer the question, Are our students learning, and how do we know?

If we really mean it when we say we are going to focus on ensuring *all* students learn, when some students experience difficulty with their learning, or demonstrate proficiency, the school would develop a schoolwide, systematic plan to provide students with additional time, support, or enrichment within the school day, regardless of the teacher to whom they are assigned.

Figure 6.1 correlates the four critical questions of learning with examples of critical tasks of collaborative teams. This figure is also helpful in depicting the interconnectedness of the work that occurs in teams that are focusing on the right things related to improving student learning levels.

---

1. **What do we expect students to learn?**

   Essential outcomes/power standards; learning targets; pacing guides

2. **How will we know if they learned it?**

   Common assessments; quick checks for understanding; collaborative analysis of student learning

3. **How do we respond when students experience difficulty in their learning?**

   Additional time and support; differentiated instruction; systematic interventions; RTI; Positive Behavior Intervention Support

4. **How do we respond when students do learn?**

   Differentiated instruction; public recognition and celebration

---

Figure 6.1: Teamwork based on the four critical questions that guide the work of a PLC.

When district leaders really mean it when they proclaim that ensuring high levels of learning for all students is the district's mission, they ensure that collaborative teams focus like a laser on the critical questions of learning. They move beyond *hoping* their students will learn, to actually collaboratively engaging in the hard work that goes with *ensuring* their students learn.

Develop Team Norms

One of the first questions each team must address is how it will go about its work and the shared commitments it is willing to make as a team. Team norms are simply agreed-upon parameters within which the team will conduct its work. All teams, not just teacher teams, must develop norms, both at the district office and individual school levels.

Again, leaders must address the *why* question. It's important that teams understand the rationale for developing norms. Ensure that teams develop shared knowledge on how collaboratively developed team norms are an effective tool for enhancing team effectiveness. If this step is overlooked—if the *why* is not understood—developing team norms will be viewed as a one-time event, a task that has to be completed, rather than as a useful tool that guides teamwork. Figures 6.2 and 6.3 (page 114) show two examples of team norms from White River.

- The primary focus of our meetings will be directed toward improving learning levels of students in the White River School District.

- All students, regardless of the particular school they attend, will be the concern of everyone on the team. We will move from a culture of "my" students to one of "our" students.

- As a team, we will anticipate potential questions, issues, and problems and collectively seek the best ways to respond.

- We will openly share learning data, always seeking to help and support each other, as well as learn from each other.

- We will practice, rehearse, and model the behaviors we are expecting of collaborative teams within our schools.

- We will engage in collective inquiry—seeking best practices as we strive to improve student learning in the White River School District.

- We will go hard on ideas and issues and soft on the people.

Figure 6.2: Sample administrative team norms.

Source: White River School District. Used with permission.

- We will meet at 7:30 a.m. sharp in room B-138. Those who will not attend the meeting should notify the group or call x5565 if there is a last-minute cancellation.

- We will dismiss on time at 8:30 a.m.

- Our focus is on improving student learning.

- To facilitate a safe environment for taking risks, our department requests prior notice if someone outside the team drops in.

- We make decisions by consensus (through discussion) and support the group's decision.

- We respect confidentiality of students and staff.

- Administration shall hear one voice representing the English department (curriculum leader).

- We will remind each other to stay on task but understand the need to be collegial.

- To facilitate participation from all members, we encourage the quiet and curb interruption, if bothersome.

- Each month, one member is designated as note-taker. This person types meeting notes in Cornell Note form and brings copies for each member to the next meeting. The note-taker also places a copy of the minutes in Greg B. and Mike H.'s boxes in the main office.

- Each member brings a PLC binder to each meeting. It should include related study articles, notes from prior meetings, power standards, other resources, and student work.

- The instructional leader sends a detailed agenda as well as room changes (if applicable) by the Thursday prior to each meeting.

Figure 6.3: Sample high school English department norms.

Source: White River School District. Used with permission.

District leadership plays a key role in the development of team norms by making resources available, providing examples, and most important, insisting that each principal ensures that teams actually develop and begin using norms. Teams should be expected to develop accountability protocols that will be followed when team members do not adhere to their team's norms. District leaders also play an important role in creating an environment where team norms are being shared within and between schools. Most important, effective district leaders constantly ask, "Are team norms being used? Do teams refer to their norms? Are team norms revisited and revised as needed?"

Just like everything else, the importance of team norms is viewed in direct proportion to the attention they receive. In this regard, the roles of the principal and team leader are critical. By monitoring the work of teams—what they are doing and how they are doing it—the effectiveness of a particular team's use of norms can be determined and enhanced. One important measure of the effectiveness of team norms is what happens when team norms are violated. While there is no one correct way to handle violations of team norms, violations must be addressed. Otherwise, the norms lose all their meaning. James McGregor Burns (1978), the Pulitzer Prize–winning historian, notes that nothing reduces a leader's credibility faster than the failure to address an obvious

> *One important measure of the effectiveness of team norms is what happens when team norms are violated. While there is no one correct way to handle violations of team norms, violations must be addressed.*

problem. Burns's admonition certainly applies to the need to address violations of team norms.

Clarify and Add Meaning to the Essential Outcomes

For teamwork to be relevant in classrooms, it's critical that teams quickly focus on student learning issues. District leaders must work with the district principal team and teacher teams to focus on the first critical question associated with improving student learning (DuFour, DuFour, Eaker, & Many, 2010), What is absolutely essential for students to learn?

In many ways, this is a rather obvious question. At White River, we approached it like this: *if we really mean it* when we say the fundamental purpose of our district is to ensure that all students learn at high levels, doesn't it make sense that we need to be crystal clear about what we expect all students to learn?

Of course, school districts rarely approach this question with a clean slate. All districts and schools already have a curriculum in place, even if the curriculum is simply a replica of the state standards. So the work of the teams is often to clarify and add *meaning* to the essential outcomes that all students would be expected to master for each subject, grade, and course. The key word here is *clarify*. Teams do not have the license to disregard state (or provincial) and district frameworks, or the state or province summative test expectations. Instead, teams become students of the standards by collaboratively clarifying what each standard means, along with the relative importance of each. Figure 6.4 (page 116) shows a sample set of essential outcomes, along with learning targets written in student-friendly language.

Power Standards (Washington Mathematics Grade Level Expectations)

3.1D Estimate sums and differences to approximate solutions to problems and determine reasonableness of answers.

3.6F Represent a problem situation using words, numbers, pictures, or symbols.

3.1A Read, write, compare, order, and represent numbers to 10,000 using numbers, words, and symbols.

Learning Targets

- I am learning to use pictures (symbols) to show number values.
- I am learning to recognize minimal collections.
- I am learning to show numbers in expanded notation. (300 + 20 + 6 = 326)
- I am learning to estimate to the nearest ten by rounding.
- I am learning to check for a reasonable answer.
- I am learning to pick an efficient (smart) strategy to solve a word problem.
- I am learning to solve two-digit addition and subtraction word problems, making my work clear and showing my thinking.
- I am learning to add two-digit numbers using regrouping.
- I am learning to add two-digit numbers using other strategies.
- I am learning to subtract two-digit numbers using regrouping.
- I am learning to subtract two-digit numbers using other strategies.

Figure 6.4: Third-grade essential outcomes in mathematics.

Source: White River School District. Used with permission.

Reduce Content

When done properly, having collaborative teams of teachers agree on the essential outcomes for each subject or course can be a powerful tool for reducing content.

Once teams begin studying content standards, it quickly becomes apparent there are more standards than the amount of time available to teachers. Also, by collaboratively discussing what is currently being taught in various classes, teachers begin to realize that some content does not relate to *any* particular standard. Also, it becomes obvious that some content is much more important than other content. Therefore, teams need to agree to teach less but more significant content at greater depth, and in more meaningful ways.

When done properly, having collaborative teams of teachers agree on the essential outcomes for each subject or course can be a powerful tool for reducing content.

The idea of reducing content also raises the issue of teachers who decide to arbitrarily teach units or lessons on topics of which they have a particular interest. For example, perhaps a teacher visited a foreign country during his summer vacation. While studying that country may be interesting, unless it is related to particular standards, valuable time is being redirected from things for which students will be held accountable. In White River, we constantly reminded everyone that (1) time is an extremely valuable and limited resource, and (2) when we use our time to teach a particular topic, that time is no longer available to teach or expand on something else.

Develop Common Pacing Guides

One of the benefits that occurs when teacher teams clarify the essential outcomes for students is that the process naturally leads to determining how much time should be devoted to each standard. For example, in

The goal is not to adhere to the pacing guide, but to make sure students master each standard.

White River, collaborative teams studied the school calendar and "chunked out" the standards, allotting time to teach each standard in a meaningful way. It is important to note that these pacing guides were *not* rigid, but rather a team's best guess about how to best use their time. Teachers were not expected to be on the same page each day! Common pacing guides should be flexible, and teachers must be urged to monitor and adjust their individual schedules as needed. The goal is not to adhere to the pacing guide, but to make sure students master each standard.

Focus on Vertical Articulation

While the initial content discussions should focus on clarifying grade level, subject-by-subject essential outcomes, there is also the need to engage faculty and staff in discussions focusing on vertical articulation between grade levels or courses. We urge district leaders to form *vertical articulation teams* in order to collaboratively analyze the standards and determine the appropriate grade-level or course divisions and the sequencing of content. Additionally, conversations within vertical teams allow the faculty to understand what will have been covered in depth the previous year, as well as what will be covered the following year or in another course. This looking "up and down" as well as "across" is an essential aspect of implementing a guaranteed and viable curriculum.

Determine Proficiency Levels

Effective teams go beyond merely agreeing on the essential outcomes and pacing for each subject, grade, or course. Leaders should direct teams to have deep, meaningful dialogue around the question, What would this standard, if met, look like in terms of student work? This is critically important because ultimately students will be asked to do something on the state summative assessments to demonstrate they are proficient. Effective collaborative teams follow this natural progression of thinking: What is the evidence we expect students to generate in order to demonstrate proficiency? What will the work of students look like if it meets the standard? And, importantly, what will be the questions and formats of our formative assessments?

Answering these questions helps teams not only sharpen their focus on the essential outcomes, but also plan more effective units, write more effective formative assessments, and provide students with appropriate practice and focused, specific feedback.

Drilling deeper doesn't end here. Teams should collaboratively agree upon *levels* of proficiency. This naturally leads to discussions around such issues as common scoring rubrics, grading, appropriate and specific homework assignments, parameters and norms for students redoing work, and shared instructional strategies as teams work collaboratively to develop high-quality unit plans.

Plan Units Collaboratively

One of the most important activities in which collaborative teams engage is unit planning. While there is no "right" way for teams to go about the task of planning instructional units, there are a number of things teams should think about and pay attention to. Figure 6.5 provides a visual depiction of essential topics teams typically address as they engage in the work of unit planning. Note that multiple checks for understanding should occur throughout the unit, including performance assessments, products scored by rubric, pencil-and-paper exercises, and observation.

Often, teachers will quickly express concern about this collaboration: "Aren't we becoming too lockstep in our approach?" "Isn't this a cookie-cutter approach?" "Whatever happened to the idea of individual teacher autonomy?" It is critical that district and school leaders continually and consistently emphasize that *teacher autonomy and creativity are not only allowed, they are encouraged*—but within a set of clearly defined parameters.

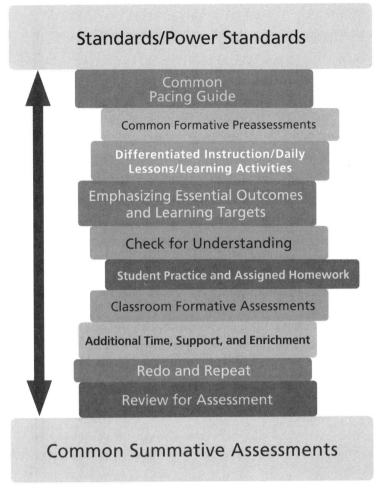

Figure 6.5: A conceptual unit planning framework for teams.

Source: Adapted from Ainsworth & Viegut (2006).

In other words, leaders must be tight regarding the collaboratively developed framework for what students should know and loose around the questions related to how teachers teach, encouraging creativity, experimentation, and research-based instructional strategies that also reflect the unique personality, background, experiences, and strengths of individual teachers.

As in unit planning, while there is no "right" way to teach, teams should engage in deep, rich discussions about instructional effectiveness. Such discussions should focus on specific aspects of effective instructional practices. Figure 6.6 (page 120) gives examples of topics that teams should discuss both before and after units have been taught.

How much should teams tackle at one time? There is no correct answer. On one hand, it only makes sense that we should be clear about what students should

1. Am I absolutely clear about what my students should know or be able to do as a result of my instruction? Were these essential outcomes the result of a collaborative effort by my team, and are they tied directly to state/provincial standards and professional/industry standards for my content area?

2. Am I clear, and are students clear, regarding the level of proficiency that is expected for each standard? Were these proficiency standards collaboratively developed by my team?

3. What will I do to preassess where my students currently are on the standards that are embedded in each unit? What is the relationship between where my students are and the instructional strategies I plan to utilize?

4. As I plan my unit or lesson, have I ensured that every student will practice, in class, the kinds of things for which they will be held accountable on the formative and summative assessments? Are they practicing things in the same formats as the formats on the assessments? How will I monitor their practice?

5. Have I used formative assessment results (both my individual assessments and the common formative assessments that have been developed by the team) to analyze learning levels student by student, skill by skill?

6. Have I identified specific homework assignments that will provide students with focused practice beyond classroom instruction?

7. Have plans been developed for students to receive additional time and support (especially focused practice) when they experience difficulty in their learning?

8. How will I extend and enrich the learning of students who demonstrate proficiency on the learning standards?

Figure 6.6: Questions for classroom instruction within a simultaneous loose-tight framework.

learn in *every* subject, grade, or course. On the other hand, there is only so much we can reasonably undertake at any given time. So, while a district or school might first only focus on mathematics or literacy, teams must understand that the same processes will ultimately be used to improve learning levels in every subject or course.

The work of clarifying what students need to know is never done. Education, especially at the state and national level, is in a constant state of flux. And as teams review student learning data from various sources, they will continually sharpen the curricular focus throughout the district.

Develop Common Formative Assessments

District leaders cannot be content with merely clarifying what students must learn. They must lead a cultural shift from an almost exclusive reliance on infrequent, high-stakes, mandated summative assessments, to a balanced approach using more frequent, collaboratively developed, common formative assessments. Students are more apt to perform well on high-stakes summative assessments if the quality of their learning has been regularly monitored along the way—especially if the results of the assessments were used to provide students with additional time, support, or enrichment.

While formative assessments take many forms, the impact of formative assessments is enhanced when teachers work collaboratively to develop *common* formative assessments. A collaborative team of teachers who share the same content develop more effective formative assessments than individual teachers working alone. As they develop their assessments, teachers grapple with questions such as, What did we say we want students to learn? What did we define as demonstrating proficiency? In what formats should assessments be written? Have we addressed the taxonomy of learning? How will we score the assessments? The most important question to consider, however, is, How will we analyze and use the results of the assessments to provide students with appropriate, specific, and focused additional time and support or enrichment, as well as improve our own instructional practices?

Get Started

At virtually every stop on the journey to becoming a professional learning community, districts are faced with the tendency to wait, to postpone, until the time is right.

> *We urge district leaders not to let their quest for perfection keep them from getting started.*

There is almost always the persistent feeling that you're not quite ready to begin. This is certainly true when it comes to asking collaborative teams to develop and use common formative assessments. We urge district leaders not to let their quest for perfection keep them from getting started. The fact is, teams learn how to write really good formative assessments by first doing the work and then getting better.

As White River leaders began the work of engaging teams in writing common formative assessments, they started from this assumption: when students take a high-stakes summative assessment, it should not be the first time they see questions in a particular format. Students should feel confident that they have mastered the required content and skills, and confident that they will not be surprised by the format of the assessment questions. To this end, collaborative teams worked to improve the quality of their formative assessments incrementally by learning everything they could about the formats of questions on various summative assessments their students would be taking.

Improve Assessment Literacy

The format of high-stakes assessment questions is important, but there may be deeper assessment issues that teams need to study. Districts who engage collaborative teams in writing common formative assessments often recognize early that the knowledge base regarding the appropriate and significant role of assessment varies greatly among faculty and staff.

In White River, the district leadership recognized the importance of modeling the PLC way of thinking by directing a small guiding coalition to seek out and collaboratively learn about best assessment practices. Initially, this simply involved shared reading and discussion. Common reading and discussions helped provide the administration, faculty, and staff across the district with a basic shared vocabulary. To promote a deeper understanding of best assessment practices, the district leadership arranged for an assessment expert to conduct assessment literacy training. These activities helped administration, faculty, and staff gain an appreciation and understanding of the powerful role formative assessments can play in improving student learning.

Even when collaborative teams gain an understanding of common formative assessments and experience training from assessment experts, however, there often remains an uneasiness about exactly how to develop common formative assessments and how to use the results, as well as concern about how the administration might use the results. Also, there often is the lingering question as to whether developing common formative assessments will *really* make a significant difference in student learning. The fact is there is nothing leaders can say on the front end that will convince everyone of the efficacy of common formative assessments. This will only occur as student learning data reflect improvement. Data can have a powerful influence on opinion. Commitment follows experience; it doesn't precede it.

The language of assessment can sometimes be a barrier to gaining a deep understanding of assessment concepts and practices. Make a conscious effort to use examples and analogies that help teachers understand the practical aspects of formative assessment. For example, we often use high school sports as an example of how the practice of collaborative teams utilizing formative assessment data to make sure students are prepared already occurs regularly in virtually every high school in North America. Every coaching staff utilizes the practice of scrimmaging prior to a game; then coaching staffs (a collaborative team of teachers) collaboratively analyze the results of these scrimmages in order to make adjustments *prior* to the game. The performing arts are another great analogy. In our work with schools, we often ask faculty and staff to reflect on this question: Prior to the public performance of a high school play, what typically happens in order to ensure everyone knows his or her lines and is confident in what to do? Someone usually quickly responds, "Dress rehearsal!" Take the mystery out of assessment by helping collaborative teams think of common formative assessments as academic scrimmages or dress rehearsals.

One of the most effective ways collaborative teams can improve the quality of their common assessments is simply by sharing and learning from each other. District leaders can create opportunities in which teams share their common assessments and discuss issues they were facing as well as their successes in developing effective ways

> *Take the mystery out of assessment by helping collaborative teams think of common formative assessments as academic scrimmages or dress rehearsals.*

to monitor the learning of individual students, skill by skill. We also urge district leaders to utilize resources from neighboring districts that have successfully embedded collaborative teaming in their schools. In the White River School District, when teams began the task of collaboratively developing common formative assessments, teams from a neighboring district spent a day sharing how they developed and utilized common formative assessments, as well as some examples of the assessments they developed. Teachers helping teachers is a powerful and underutilized resource. Teachers place a lot of confidence in testimony from their peers, and rightfully so.

Collaboratively Analyze Student Work

Quite obviously, simply having collaborative teams develop common formative assessments will do little, if anything, to improve student learning. How teams analyze and then use the results of the assessments is what really matters in terms of affecting student learning. Effective district leaders work to ensure that teams use collaborative analysis of student learning data to make decisions about additional time,

> *Simply having collaborative teams develop common formative assessments will do little, if anything, to improve student learning. How teams analyze and then use the results of the assessments is what really matters in terms of affecting student learning.*

support, or enrichment for students; improve their own instructional practices; and improve their effectiveness as a team.

At White River, we wanted teams to bring more than student learning data to the table for analysis. We wanted them to also bring student work. This was important because students with the same test scores may have missed different problems or parts of problems. While each team developed its own "personality" or way of doing things, the things teams did as they collaboratively analyzed student learning data were consistent across the district.

For example, when teams first looked at the results of a common formative assessment, one of the initial things they worked to determine, often by a simple item analysis, was the learning patterns of the entire group of students who were given the assessment. What strengths were evident? In what areas did students struggle? What learning gaps were evident? Effective teams engage in rich discussions about the data patterns, speculating what instructional strategies were the most successful, which things need to be taught differently, what content needs additional attention, and how the assessment could be improved.

Individual teachers also analyze the data pertaining to their particular classroom, again asking, "What strengths are evident? In what areas did students struggle?" Teachers drill deeper to examine the learning data of each student, skill by skill. Most important, in a professional learning community, teachers share learning data and student work with each other. They view all the students—even those who are not in their specific class—as "our kids." By collaboratively analyzing student learning data, teams develop a culture in which they hold themselves mutually accountable for the learning of all students who receive instruction from team members.

District leaders and principals must also engage in analysis of student work. In White River, principals meet every six to eight weeks, accompanied by either a teacher team or team leader, for a districtwide data meeting. They share specific pieces of student learning data on requested topics (for example, algebra I, expository writing, and so on). This allows the district leadership team to determine whether students are learning *before* receiving the results of the state summative assessment. There are specific protocols for the meeting, and as with other major activities associated with implementing PLC practices, the Deputy Superintendent for Teaching and Learning (Janel) sent an email to everyone explaining the protocols and why these districtwide data meetings were important. (See page 184 in the appendix for a sample email: "Why Data Meetings?")

Figure 6.7 shows a two-page form used in White River to guide the work of collaborative teams as they analyze student learning data from common formative assessments.

School _____ Grade _____

Subject Area _____ Name of Assessment _____

5 min	Power standards or learning targets measured:
5 min	In what areas did our students do well on this assessment?
5 min	What instructional strategies helped our students do well? (Skip this question if you are using a preassessment.)
5 min	What skill deficiencies do we see?
5 min	What patterns do we see in the mistakes, and what do they tell us?
5 min	Which students did not master essential standards and will need additional time and support?
20 min	What intervention will be provided to address unlearned skills, and how will we check for success?
5 min	Do we need to tweak or improve this assessment?
10 min	Which students mastered standards, and what is our plan for extending and enriching their learning?

	Class 1	Class 2	Class 3	Class 4
Total Students				
Intensive Support				
Strategic Support				
Approaching Standard				
Meeting Standard				

Figure 6.7: Team common assessment analysis worksheet.　　Continued➜

Source: White River School District. Used with permission.

Visit **go.solution-tree.com/plcbooks** to download a reproducible version of this figure.

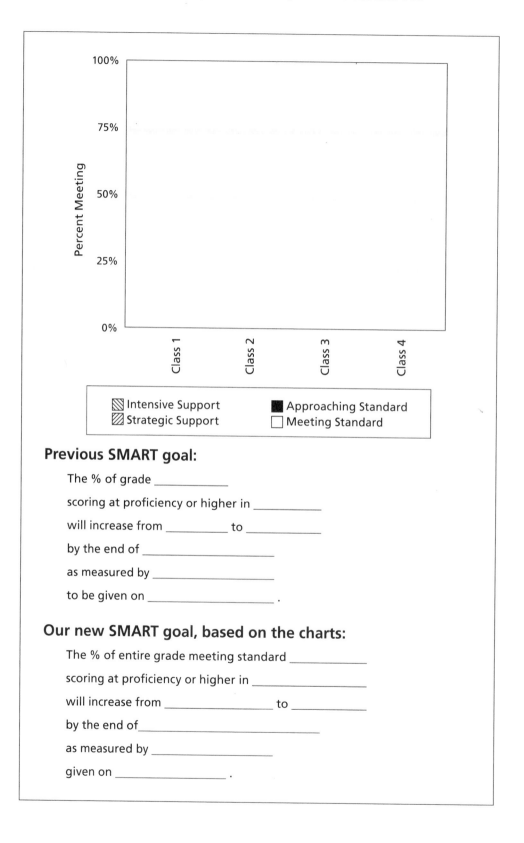

Previous SMART goal:

The % of grade _____

scoring at proficiency or higher in _____

will increase from _____ to _____

by the end of _____

as measured by _____

to be given on _____ .

Our new SMART goal, based on the charts:

The % of entire grade meeting standard _____

scoring at proficiency or higher in _____

will increase from _____ to _____

by the end of_____

as measured by _____

given on _____ .

Use Student Learning Data

Of course, even collaboratively analyzing learning data will do little to improve student performance levels. District leaders must guarantee the connection between collaboratively analyzing student learning and the utilization of specific, focused intervention plans to provide students with additional time, support, or enrichment. This is perhaps the single most critical connection that collaborative teams must make. If teams do everything else well, but fail to analyze *and act* on student learning data—student by student, skill by skill—they will make little impact on student learning.

In more traditional districts, the quantity and quality of support or enrichment students receive is left to the discretion of individual teachers. District leaders seeking to reculture their schools into professional learning communities must engage every school in the development of a plan that provides layered assistance or enrichment to students within the school day, regardless of the teacher to whom they were assigned. Districts must send a consistent message that this will be required. (See page 186 in the appendix for a sample districtwide email on this topic: "Additional Time and Support for Adults in a Professional Learning Community.")

We constantly, and rather forcefully, remind district leaders that the degree to which districts successfully improve learning levels depends on the *quality* of individual school plans for providing students with additional time and support when they experience difficulty in their learning, as well as extension and enrichment when they demonstrate proficiency.

What We Have Learned About Ensuring a Focus on Student Learning

Chapter 5 explored some of the critical steps leadership can to take to ensure that teams are effective, but in our work with schools and districts, we have observed some steps that help teams focus specifically on student learning.

Consider Reporting Issues

Various issues will arise as collaborative teams become deeply engaged in doing the work associated with an intense and passionate focus on learning. Frequently, faculty and staff will begin to question traditional practices associated with homework, grading, and reporting pupil progress. It is not unusual for someone within a more traditional school to point out the need to change the district's report card format to a more standards-based approach. The graphic in figure 6.8 (page 128) helps communicate the point that changing the report card only makes sense after the prerequisite work associated with a focus on learning has been addressed.

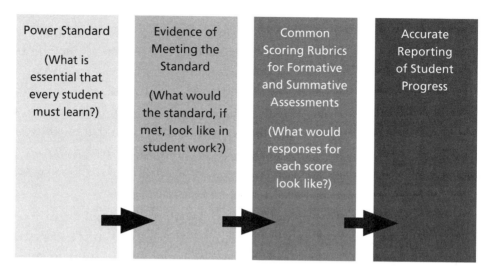

| Power Standard (What is essential that every student must learn?) | Evidence of Meeting the Standard (What would the standard, if met, look like in student work?) | Common Scoring Rubrics for Formative and Summative Assessments (What would responses for each score look like?) | Accurate Reporting of Student Progress |

Figure 6.8: Prerequisite collaborative planning for standards-based progress reporting.

Address the Schedule

Districts will not be able to provide high-quality time, support, and enrichment within the school day, regardless of the teacher to whom students were assigned, unless schools are willing to adjust class schedules. One of the most common barriers that faculty and staff cite as they discuss ways to provide students with additional time, support, and enrichment is, "But the schedule won't allow it." Some principals will find this task to be very difficult simply because they try to solve this problem by themselves. Instead, they should do what those in professional learning communities do—put together a small guiding coalition to help with the task. The group should start by gaining shared knowledge—learning how other schools have solved this problem.

District leadership must send the clear and consistent message that changes in the school schedule that are designed to increase collaboration and provide students with additional time, support, and enrichment will not only be supported but are *expected*.

Define Quality Standards for Additional Time, Support, and Enrichment

We know from experience that if district leaders simply direct each school to develop plans for additional time, support, and enrichment, the quality of the plans more than likely will vary greatly. Therefore, we urge districts to utilize the criteria for support and enrichment that DuFour, DuFour, Eaker, and Many (2010) present in *Learning by Doing* as the basis for standards of quality that each school's plan will be expected to meet—an excellent example of loose-tight leadership. That is, although plans will vary from school to school, at a minimum each plan should be collaboratively developed and written, widely shared, systematic, flexible, timely, and directive. Figure 6.9 shows a rubric the White River School District created to outline the parameters and improve the quality of individual school plans for additional time and support across the district.

1. The plan should be collaboratively developed and systematic, meaning that the plan should be a school plan that includes interventions first at the classroom level, then the team level, and then schoolwide. The primary focus of the plan should be interventions and enrichment that occur within the school day, regardless of the teacher to whom the students are assigned.

2. The plan should be in writing and widely circulated.

3. The plan should be timely—providing students with appropriate and meaningful time, support, or enrichment early in the school year, certainly no later than after the first three weeks of school.

4. The plan should be directive rather than invitational. That is, the plan should direct students to the appropriate intervention or enrichment strategy rather than simply encourage them to do so.

5. The plan should be flexible, allowing students to move in and out of intervention and enrichment.

6. The plan should be periodically monitored for effectiveness and adapted accordingly. Remember, the goal is to improve student learning, not merely to develop a plan.

Figure 6.9: Sample rubric for effective school plans for additional time, support, and enrichment.

Source: White River School District; adapted from DuFour & Eaker (1998).

Seek Best Practice

Examples are a powerful way to start. District leaders first should build shared knowledge by seeking high-quality examples of plans for additional time, support, and enrichment from external sources such as *Raising the Bar and Closing the Gap: Whatever It Takes* (DuFour, DuFour, Eaker, & Karhanek, 2010) as well as examples from other schools and districts (see www.allthingsplc.info). While it is not advisable to simply transfer any of these plans into your school, examples serve as a powerful way to help faculty and staff see the work and learn together how others have approached the task.

District leaders need not look only outside the district for best practices. Within every district, many best practices will already be in place in certain schools and classrooms. In White River, principals and faculty members started by sharing practices that they were already doing to provide students with additional time, support, and enrichment. Not only was this a good way to get started, but it also provided a way to honor the good work that was already taking place within the district.

Encourage Reflection

In many ways a professional learning community is a culture of reflection. Continuous improvement is only possible when we stop to reflect on what we've done, how it worked, and what we'll do next time. Figure 6.10 shows a tool, developed by Adam Uhler, the principal of Mountain Meadow Elementary School, to assist collaborative teams in reflecting about units of instruction. Note that teams are instructed to turn in completed forms to the principal; by monitoring the team's

---

At the end of each math and writing unit, please take time (20 minutes) to reflect on student learning during the unit. The questions are meant to guide your conversation. Please turn in the end-of-unit reflection to the principal within a week of the end of the unit.

1. What was your team's goal? Share a brief (1–3 sentences) rationale.

2. What were your team's results? How did kids do compared to the goal? Why?

   • How many kids are below benchmark? Who are they (list them)? What is the team's plan for intervention?

   • Please include a sample of work from one high, midrange, and low proficiency student.

3. How has this information influenced your practice? What are the next steps for your below, at, or above proficiency students?

4. What is the focus for the next unit? How is it tied to the previous and following unit?

5. What did you learn as a team from the process? The following guiding questions are points to consider. You may not need to address all of them.

   • What are the strategies/supplements/other items that worked well that we want to remember to do again next time we teach this unit?

   • What are some strategies/supplements/other items that did not work well that we would either discard or revise when we teach this again?

   • What did we learn about pacing this unit?

6. What other notes do we want to record for future reference on this unit?

Figure 6.10: Sample end-of-unit reflection guide.

Source: Adam Uhler. Used with permission.

efforts to reflect on their work (not just asking teams to reflect), he signals to all that reflection is valued in a professional learning community.

Monitor and Adjust Interventions and Enrichment

Although most faculty and staff support the *concept* of providing additional time, support, and enrichment to students, there is usually great reluctance to actually develop and implement a plan. Many faculty and staff pose legitimate concerns and issues, but it is simply impossible to satisfactorily address everyone's concerns prior to actually implementing a plan.

In White River, we urged district leaders to address this issue by making a sincere commitment to the faculty and staff that the district would not wait until the end of the year to make necessary adjustments, but rather would continually seek feedback, and monitor and adjust plans as they were being implemented. This single commitment relieved a tremendous amount of anxiety, since faculty and staff realized they would not be stuck with something that wasn't working. It is important to note that while district leaders made the commitment to monitor and adjust the plans for additional time, support, and enrichment, whether each school would develop a plan was not open for discussion.

Reflections

A professional learning community requires a structural and cultural shift from a focus on teaching and covering content to a focus on high levels of student learning for each and every student. The central question, then, is to what degree your district or school has made this fundamental shift.

Individually or in teams, reflect on questions such as the following.

1. Have collaborative teams collaboratively clarified the essential outcomes for every subject, grade, or course?

2. Are these outcomes aligned with state or provincial and district standards, as well as various high-stakes summative assessments?

3. Have teams engaged in a process designed to reduce content in order that more significant content can be taught in greater depth, in more significant ways?

4. How has the issue of vertical articulation between grades or courses been addressed?

5. Have teams developed guides to ensure that adequate time is available for teaching essential outcomes?

6. How are essential outcomes updated and revised as needed?

7. Have collaborative teams engaged in a process to develop common formative assessments in order to monitor the learning of students on a frequent and timely basis?

8. Are the formats of the formative assessments consistent with high-stakes summative assessments?

Chapter 7

Ensuring Adult Learning

A focus on learning in a professional learning community isn't just for students. Leaders in professional learning communities recognize that the quality of student learning is greatly affected by the quality of adult learning throughout the district. As a teacher in White River once observed, "If the adults don't get it, how can we expect the students to get it?" District leaders must realize that if they really mean it when they proclaim ensuring high levels of student learning as the district's core purpose, they must focus on ensuring deep learning for the adults in the district as well—and that deep learning will most likely occur when the adults learn by doing.

There is a lot of common sense to the notion that we learn best by doing, yet many districts seek to train their way to school improvement. In addressing the question of how organizations can best close the gap between what they know and what they do, Pfeffer and Sutton (2000) offer this prescription: "The answer to the knowing-doing problem is deceptively simple: Embed more of the process of acquiring new knowledge in the actual doing of the task and less in the formal training programs that are frequently ineffective. If you do it, then you will know it" (p. 27). DuFour, DuFour, and Eaker (2008) echo the call for job-embedded adult learning. They write:

> *The message is consistent and clear. The best professional development occurs in a social and collaborative setting rather than in isolation, is ongoing and sustained rather than infrequent and transitory, is job-embedded rather than external, occurs in the context of the real work of the school*

and classroom rather than in off-site workshops and courses, focuses on results (that is, evidence of improved student learning) rather than activities or prescriptions, and is systematically aligned with school and district goals rather than random. In short, the best professional development takes place in professional learning communities. (p. 370)

Apply the Critical Questions of Learning

Again, we urge districts to view the learning of adults through the lens of the classroom. That is, best practices in classrooms also apply to the professional learning of adults; the district is simply a bigger classroom.

Planning for adult learning from this perspective enables district leaders to focus on the right things. In more traditional district cultures, the focus is often on planning activities. Questions such as What would be a good in-service activity for our next professional development day? and Who would be a speaker the faculty and staff would enjoy hearing? are common. In districts with which we have worked, we have seen the efficacy of asking critical questions about adult learning that mirror the questions that impact student learning.

What Do We Want the Adults to Learn?

In White River, we worked to build a system of teams. This raised the question, what do we want teams to learn? The process of planning for adult learning should mirror the process of teacher teams; begin by collaboratively clarifying the learning expectations. Decisions about the focus of professional learning should be based on information that flows directly from the work of collaborative teams *and should be chosen specifically to increase the capacity of teams and individual teachers to more effectively impact student learning.*

For example, as White River engaged in building shared knowledge of all staff in such areas as assessment literacy, the administrative team quickly realized the need to differentiate the professional development of the faculty and staff team by team. Each team, working with its principal, identified the specific needs of students, the needs and work of the team, and the different time options to do the work.

Figure 7.1 shows a sample planning form for a fourth-grade team that has identified the general area of writing as a focus of concern, specifically elaboration and the use of thinking charts as tools for elaboration. The left column prompts the team to define areas of work for each month, and the headings across the top prompt the team to identify when the work will be done and who will be

When	Identified Area	Team Time	Half Days	Dispersed Leadership
August–September What are we seeing in student work? What evidence does the common formative assessment give us?				
October What are we seeing in student work? What evidence does the common formative assessment give us?				
November What are we seeing in student work? What evidence does the common formative assessment give us?				

Figure 7.1: Sample professional development plan for a fourth-grade team.

Source: White River School District. Used with permission.

responsible for leading the effort. When completing this form, team members will identify how they will use the time the district has allotted for teams to build shared knowledge. For example, the fourth-grade team has several hours of team time when members will plan their writing units and analyze the results of the first common assessment in writing. There is also a half day of training in late September when the team will be involved in the work of aligning K–5 writing across the district. The team will work with the principal and district-level leaders to identify who will lead the training. For example, training may be provided by a consultant, a member of the team, a member of a team from another school, or perhaps a staff member from the district office.

How Will We Know if They Have Learned It?

Again, if we seek to view adult professional learning as if the district is just a bigger classroom, it becomes self-evident that we cannot wait until the end of the year to assess the effectiveness of professional development. Instead, district leaders must ask, "If we know what we want the adults in the district to know and be able to do, how will we know if they have learned, and how can we gather this information of a frequent and timely basis?"

In White River, these questions are addressed in a number of ways, the primary way being analysis of products the teams produce. However, examining products that have been developed by teams is part of a broader approach. Consider this example: the teams across the district observed that their students were struggling to elaborate in expository and narrative writing. Elaboration is an essential skill and must be evident in student writing to meet the standard on the state assessment. As a result of what teams observed in their student work, teams were provided professional development on elaboration strategies to include the use of sensory description, anecdotes, character emotion and description, setting description, similes and metaphors, and tier II vocabulary.

> *Rather than asking the usual, "How did you like the training?," a professional learning community asks, "What has been the impact on student learning?"*

Teams then used these instructional strategies in their writing lessons with their students. Team SMART goals were also crafted to measure elaboration. When teams scored the writing papers together, they specifically looked for evidence of layered elaboration in the student writing.

As a district, White River is constantly asking, "Is there evidence that the training provided to the teachers is making a difference in student learning? Are more *kids* learning more as a result of *adults* learning more?" Make sure you ask teams the right question. Rather than asking the usual, "How did you like the training?," a professional learning community asks, "What has been the impact on student learning?"

What Support or Enrichment Will We Provide?

Providing additional time, support, and enrichment for adults is a critical component of ensuring professional learning. Adults, like students, learn at different rates and in different ways, and as they work collaboratively together, different strengths and needs will emerge. We urge districts to approach professional learning through the framework of differentiated teaming. That is, just as students receive differentiated instruction to meet unique learning needs, so too do teams need professional development that is individualized to the learning needs of teachers and teams.

For example, at White River High School, decisions about professional development experiences for teachers are based on thoughtful analysis of student learning data. When student learning data revealed that students were struggling with solving one-step and two-step equations, the algebra team realized it needed an alternate instructional method that was both tactile and concrete. District leaders provided professional development in the use of algebra tiles. The team also learned how to use algebra tiles in other areas in which many students struggled, such as combining like terms, factoring polynomials, and adding and subtracting positive and negative numbers.

Individuals also need enrichment. In many districts, teachers are left alone to develop as professionals. Figure 7.2 (page 138) depicts the stages of professional growth and development that faculty and staff in the White River School District experience during their career. Not only are teachers in White River encouraged to seek National Board Certification, they are provided assistance in a number of ways ranging from financial support to group mentoring by colleagues who have successfully completed the process. The point is this: in White River there is a clear path that moves teachers from hiring and induction into the district culture, through continuous job-embedded professional development, and ultimately National Board Certification.

Support Principal Learning

Teachers are not the only educators who work and learn in isolation. The most successful districts with which we have worked place a great deal of emphasis on the professional development of principals—they ensure that the adult learning of principals enhances the effectiveness of collaborative teams within their schools, thus improving student learning.

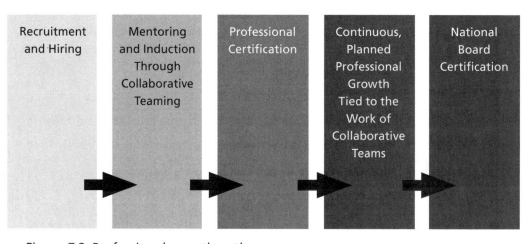

| Recruitment and Hiring | Mentoring and Induction Through Collaborative Teaming | Professional Certification | Continuous, Planned Professional Growth Tied to the Work of Collaborative Teams | National Board Certification |

Figure 7.2: Professional growth path.

Source: White River School District. Used with permission.

The work of principals changes dramatically when schools function as professional learning communities, particularly in the area of professional learning. Principals have a major responsibility to enhance the capacity of collaborative teams—they must continually strive to increase the effectiveness of each team.

Therefore, they must ensure that team members are engaged in collaborative processes that are most likely to impact student learning. In our work with school districts, we have found that the quality of professional learning within principal teams impacts the quality of professional learning in teacher teams, and the quality of work of collaborative teams is directly linked to the leadership capacity of building principals. Therefore, ensuring the professional learning of principals is a critical responsibility of a district that seeks to function as a professional learning community.

In White River, we learned we first had to clarify what we expected principals to do; then organize them into teams so that they could learn and grow together; and finally provide them with the resources, training, support, and importantly, examples they needed to be successful.

Practice and Rehearse Teamwork

As we have noted earlier, one of the most important assumptions that should drive the professional learning of adults in a school district is this: the work of the principal learning teams at the district level should precede and mirror the work of the learning leadership teams in each school, and this work should focus explicitly on the work that is expected of individual collaborative teams. Engaging principal teams in practicing and rehearsing the work that is expected of teacher teams enhances the likelihood of team success. Practicing and rehearsing the work of teacher teams not only trains principals to assist the teams within their buildings, it increases their credibility with teachers since they have done and can model the work themselves.

For example, suppose leaders realize that some teacher teams struggle with going beyond merely understanding what particular state standards mean and defining what each standard, if met, would look like in student work. In this situation, it is important that principals are able to assist teams that are confused or need clarification. In order to make sure principals gain

Practicing and rehearsing the work of teacher teams not only trains principals to assist the teams within their buildings, it increases their credibility with teachers since they have done and can model the work themselves.

a deep, rich understanding of what this practice looks like before they are asked for help, the principal team can examine sample state standards and practice converting state standards into student-friendly "I can" statements. By wrestling with the process themselves, principals become better equipped to help others. This is a classic example of both learning by doing as well as the importance of leaders first practicing and rehearsing the work that is expected of others.

Focus on Results

Just as for students, professional learning for adults requires systems of accountability. To develop a culture of accountability for adult learning, districts must confront the disconnect that often exists between what is expected and the quality of work that is ultimately accepted (Eaker & Keating, 2008). This expectations-acceptance gap is particularly prevalent in adults' professional learning. Districts should clarify standards related to high-quality adult learning and insist that the work mirror the standards—even if it means the work must be redone. A collaboratively developed quality standard for adult professional learning is an important tool for improving the quality of work throughout the district.

In the White River School District, we quickly discovered the expectations-acceptance gap: the significant gap between what the district said it expected and what it was willing to accept. For example, most principals were required to work with their teams to craft a written learning improvement plan, in the belief that a well-implemented plan would have a positive impact on student learning. For years, the plans were crafted, turned in and checked off at the district office, and rarely looked at again. Results of the plan were seldom monitored by the school or the district office. Turning in school improvement plans created the *illusion of action* when it came to improving learning. When the district office started monitoring the *quality* of the plans through the lens of improving learning, however, some principals were shocked to have to redo plans that were far below expectations. We addressed their needs by again utilizing a strategy that works well in the classroom: that is, simply pull up a chair, and give specific, meaningful feedback about how to improve the quality of the work. The concept of expecting students to redo work until it meets an acceptable level of quality applies equally to the work of adults.

What We Have Learned About Ensuring Adult Learning

While each school district with which we have worked had its own unique experiences as it undertook a new approach to adult learning, some lessons about what works—and doesn't—tend to be universal.

Invitation Will Not Work

Simply encouraging adults to engage in their ongoing professional learning will not work. Inviting adults to learn will never be enough. For collaborative teams to be successful in their efforts to improve student learning, the learning of adults must be *embedded* into both the structure and culture routine of the district, and most important, reflected in the day-to-day work of each collaborative team.

Establish the *Why*

When educators are introduced to change, there is a tendency to respond by thinking, "This is just one more thing to do on top of everything else." It is helpful to address this issue by redefining the fundamental work that faculty and staff are being asked to do. Assume that by connecting the professional learning of adults directly to student learning, you will increase the likelihood that faculty and staff will see the relevance of what they are being asked to learn. (See page 186 in the appendix for a sample districtwide email on this topic: "Additional Time and Support for Adults in a Professional Learning Community." See also page 188 for a sample learning letter on how professional learning communities will enrich the isolated lives of teachers: "Professional Learning Communities and the Professional Life of Teachers.")

Teachers want their students to do well, and if they can see the connection between what they are being asked to learn and how it directly relates to their day-to-day work with students, they are much more likely to respond positively. Highlight the importance of adult learning, and send a clear signal that the district leadership will value and promote adult learning within the district.

Universal Happiness Is Not the Goal

Any number of reasons will emerge as to why administrators, faculty, and staff should not learn and work together. While these reasons must be recognized and understood, *they do not have to be accepted*. We learned the importance of consistently communicating the twin messages that (1) the fundamental purpose, the reason for being, of this district is to ensure high levels of learning for all students, and (2) we have organized into collaborative teams to work and learn together in order to achieve that purpose. There must be no equivocation and no exceptions.

While we value the happiness of adults who work in White River, we realized there will always be some people who are unhappy about something. We don't ignore their concerns, but ultimately we must always return to the fundamental decision point: is it good for kids?

Use Data to Influence Attitudes

Few things influence attitudes as much as evidence of success. When teams and schools demonstrate even small, incremental improvements in student learning—especially as a result of adult learning—it becomes increasingly difficult to argue with the impact that professional adult learning is having on student learning. Commitment comes only after positive experiences. District leaders must focus first on providing faculty and staff with high-quality, successful experiences that demonstrate a positive impact on student learning. Only after faculty and staff experience success will they become more deeply committed and excited.

Get Started, Then Get Better!

This is our constant advice to district leaders. Some leaders want to wait until conditions are right or everyone is on board before beginning the journey of cultural change. The fact is, the time will never be perfect. Not everyone will be on board. But get started anyway by organizing into collaborative teams, focusing on improving student learning, and making a passionate commitment to learn together in order to continually get better.

And once you begin your journey, recognize and celebrate the positive impact of professional learning on student learning. Terrence Deal and Allen Kennedy (1982) observe that in the absence of rituals and ceremonies, important values will lose all meaning. If district leaders profess they value high-quality adult learning and the work of collaborative teams, they must publically recognize and celebrate the best examples of adult learning when it occurs.

Monitor Agreed-Upon Standards of Quality

> *It is essential that district leaders clearly articulate standards of quality for specific work that is to be performed or products that are to be created, and then monitor and assist those involved as the work progresses.*

How can a district move away from a culture in which adults feel that the task is completed merely because it is "turned in and checked off"? The very concept of learning by doing implies doing the right things. However, even doing the right things doesn't address the question of *doing the right things well.* Therefore, it is essential that district leaders clearly articulate standards of quality for specific work that is to be performed or products that are to be created, and then monitor and assist those involved as the work progresses. Monitoring and feedback can have a tremendous impact on the quality of adult learning in a district that has adopted the philosophy of learning by doing.

Reflections

The quality of student learning is directly linked to the quality of adult learning, and the quality of adult learning is not left to chance in a professional learning community.

Individually or in teams, reflect on questions such as the following.

1. Does your district have a written, comprehensive plan designed to improve the quality of adult learning in order to positively impact the quality of student learning?

2. Does your district's professional development plan emphasize job-embedded adult learning? That is, does the plan connect professional development with the actual, day-to-day work of adults in the district?

3. Is the professional learning of administrators, especially principals, linked directly to the professional learning of faculty and staff? In other words, are principals learning how to do the work they are expecting others to ultimately perform?

4. Are successful professional development activities recognized and publically celebrated?

5. Are adequate resources allocated for adult learning?

6. How is the quality of professional development in your district monitored?

7. What changes do you think should be made in your district in order to significantly improve the quality of adult learning?

Chapter 8

Assessing District Progress

The journey to becoming a professional learning community is just that—a journey! Furthermore, it is a difficult, complex, and incremental journey that affects virtually every aspect of district and school culture. While there is no single right way to reculture a district into a professional learning community, as preceding chapters have shown, there are definite beliefs, concepts, and practices that *must* be embedded into the day-to-day work life of the entire district.

This raises a number of significant questions: Where are we on our journey to becoming a professional learning community? How well are we doing? Are more students learning at higher levels as a result of our efforts? What should be our next steps?

A recurring theme of this book has been that district and school leaders can enhance their effectiveness by thinking of themselves as highly successful classroom teachers. Nowhere is this analogy more relevant than in the need to frequently monitor progress at the district level. If effective classroom teachers and collaborative teams utilize the power of both formative and summative assessments, shouldn't district leaders model the same behavior when assessing progress on the PLC journey? District leaders should develop a formative assessment plan in order to periodically assess their progress on the professional learning community journey throughout the year, as well as conduct a broader, more in-depth, summative assessment annually.

Collaboratively Develop a Plan

In White River, the plan to assess progress was both formative and summative. Throughout the year, district leaders and principals monitored the quality of the work of collaborative teams, primarily through observation, discussion, and examination of team products. Most important, district leaders, principals, and teams monitored the impact on student learning on an ongoing basis.

However, district leaders recognized the need for a more formal summative assessment that would serve as an in-depth annual summary report, not only to administrators, faculty, and staff, but also to the board of education and the larger community. With the assistance of Robert Eaker, the Deputy Superintendent and a small group of district and school leaders collaboratively developed a district plan for an annual summative assessment. The plan for this summative assessment was designed to achieve four distinct purposes:

1. The plan would provide an accurate snapshot of the district's current reality. An analysis of student learning data, perceptual data, and products and artifacts would take place each spring, near the end of the school year. Team leaders, principals, and district office staff each played a role in the collection and compiling of data and artifacts.

2. The purpose of the plan would be clearly communicated; that is, to enable district and school leaders to make wise decisions, ensure that the district headed in the right direction, and focus all staff on the right next steps.

3. The plan would model the practices, commitment, and quality that were expected of others.

4. Most important, the plan would provide information regarding the degree to which the district's efforts were positively affecting student learning.

Analyze Student Learning Data

With the emphasis we have placed on embedding professional learning community concepts and practices throughout a district, it would be easy to conclude that the mission of a district should be to become a professional learning community. While districts *should* seek to function as a truly effective professional learning community, the professional learning community framework is simply a proven vehicle for enabling educators to achieve their *true* mission of ensuring high levels of student learning for all students—and adults alike.

One of the primary benefits of a comprehensive plan to assess district progress is that it helps move the culture from one that asks, "How do you *like* what we're doing?," to a results-orientated culture that asks, *"Are more students learning more?"* Therefore, an in-depth analysis of student learning patterns was the central component of White District's plan to assess progress in ongoing formative ways, and also the central component of the summative assessment of progress.

It is important to note that the analysis of learning data in the summative assessment *did not require additional testing*, but rather a *meta-analysis of existing data patterns*. For example, data such as these were examined:

- Distribution of grades—all subjects, in all grade levels, and in each course

- State assessment results

- Results from criterion-referenced common formative assessments

- Results from norm-referenced summative assessments such as the ACT, SAT, and a variety of advanced placement examinations

- Graduation rate

Add Meaning to Student Learning Data

Data collection was simply the first step in our efforts to assess White River's progress. Data in and of themselves do not *inform*. The critical task of district and school leaders is to determine what the data *mean*. For us, this involved identifying patterns, understanding perceptions, and gaining valuable insights. Although our plan for assessing progress was data driven, the ultimate value of our plan was in the *meaning* derived from collaborative analysis of the data.

For White River, *comparisons* were the primary means for adding meaning to data. For example, the first question that was addressed usually when completing the summative assessment was, Did we do better than last year? We also sought comparisons with other districts and schools within Pierce County, which contains fifteen districts, and districts of like size and demographic in Washington State, as well as national comparisons where data were available.

We also analyzed anomalies—student achievement data that stood out. For example, there may be a high failure rate in a particular course or with regards to a particular standard. These anomalies were delved into primarily through deep discussions with teacher teams.

> *Data in and of themselves do not* inform. *The critical task of district and school leaders is to determine what the data* mean.

The same emphasis on examining comparisons and anomalies of student learning data applied to both formative assessment of student learning throughout the year, as well as the annual summative assessment. These formative checks allowed for instant corrections. For example, when the geometry team at the high school sought to explain a rather wide range of grades among team members, even though they had planned the unit of instruction together, they realized they had failed to agree on appropriate homework assignments. Some teachers assigned homework that was more clearly geared directly to the standard than others. This discovery led the geometry team to include discussion about appropriate homework assignments in their future unit planning discussions. Teachers also found that they were scoring the assessments differently—giving points for different things. This led for the need to score the assessments together to ensure that they were absolutely clear on what they expected from their students, item by item, and how the assessments would be scored.

Bringing data to the table requires more than examining the numbers of test scores.

This kind of deep analysis of anomalies in learning data led the third-grade team at Mountain Meadow Elementary School to start bringing student work to team meetings when collaboratively analyzing the results of common formative assessments. The team had realized that even though students might be missing the same problems, they weren't necessarily missing the same *parts* of problems. By bringing the actual student work to the meeting, teachers could see *where and how* individual students were making mistakes rather than merely noting they arrived at the wrong answer.

Bringing data to the table requires more than examining the numbers of test scores. The third-grade team members, for example, always brings their spreadsheets with numbers to examine, discuss, and look for trends, but when they need to get down to skills that learners are actually stumbling on, they always go back to the student work they've brought along. If they need to tailor instruction to meet the needs of learners, they will dig in and make sure they are clear regarding the specific skill or skills that are causing students difficulty. For example, they might have a short formative assessment in math to see how their learners are doing with the subtraction regrouping algorithm. They look at their numbers and see that fifteen learners missed question three. If they didn't examine the student work, they might fall into the trap of one-size-fits-all intervention. Instead, they pull out those students' work and see that some students just made basic subtraction errors but understood the regrouping algorithm, while others didn't understand how to regroup across a zero. Some students struggled with both. As the teachers decide how to address these issues as a team, their work will center on creating targeted learning opportunities for each type of error rather than lumping all students who missed the same question into one intervention group.

Since the assessment plan for the district was both formative and summative, virtually everyone was involved in one way or another—especially with the formative assessments. The compiling of the summative assessment was the responsibility of the district office leaders, with principals and team leaders also supplying information and insight.

Apply Data to Decision Making

Ultimately, the value of an effective plan for assessing progress is its use in making decisions. Recall that one purpose of the White River assessment plan was to support *improved decision making*. We realized that if we didn't examine the data, we would simply be guessing about what to do next. We used the conclusions of our assessment plan in at least three ways.

1. **Determining next steps:** Once we gained a clear understanding of our current reality, we could then plan where we should go next. We knew that a thorough assessment of our district's progress would better enable us to set realistic and attainable goals. Clear, concise goals that are frequently referred to and monitored can be a valuable tool for clearly articulating the next steps in the district's efforts to enhance student learning.

   For example, as a result of White River's first year of developing a districtwide annual progress report, decisions were made to monitor and improve the work of teams more closely. Analysis of the survey data, interviews, and team products revealed that some teams had not developed or were not utilizing team norms. Additionally, district leaders learned that the quality of the products teams were developing ranged dramatically—from very good to very poor. This was especially true of the formative assessments that had been developed. The decision was made to provide more attention and training for teams that were struggling with developing and using common formative assessments.

   The analysis of progress data also raised a concern regarding the effectiveness of each school's plan for providing additional time, support, and enrichment. As a result, each principal was directed to lead a review of his or her school plan, making sure the plan met the quality rubric that was provided. The district then monitored plans for the following questions:

   - Is the plan collaboratively developed, systematic, timely, directional, and flexible?

   - Is it continually monitored for effectiveness? How?

- Does it provide time, support, and enrichment student by student, skill by skill?

2. **Conducting a structural analysis:** In White River we asked, "What changes in our structure do we need to consider that will enable us to function more effectively as a professional learning community in order to improve student learning?" Structure can be defined as policies, procedures, rules, organizational charts, role definitions, and so on (see chapter 4 for more on this). We used the information gained from assessing our progress to ensure that the formal organizational structure was compatible with and supported the district's efforts to improve student learning. For example, we asked questions such as:

  - Do we need to change our administrator performance assessment processes, our teacher observation format and practices, and our overall teacher evaluation procedure?

  - What about our professional development planning process?

  - Our hiring processes?

  - The way we allocate resources?

  - Our organizational chart?

  These are but a few of the structural issues we addressed from an analysis of progress assessment data.

3. **Analyzing district day-to-day operations:** We realized we could not simply *organize* the district into a professional learning community. We knew that while our structure was important, in and of itself, it was not enough. We paid attention to the district and school culture—the "way things are done." An analysis of the conclusions of our plan assisted us in addressing such questions as:

  - What signals do we send that communicate what we really care about in this district and in our schools?

  - What trumps learning?

  - What behaviors are we modeling?

  - What do we check on for quality?

  - What are we willing to confront—with both students and adults?

  - What questions are we struggling to answer?

  - What is the focus of our meetings? Do we have too many meetings? Are they productive?

  - Are we all on the same page, going in the same direction, with the same overarching purpose?

These are but a few of the questions the conclusions of our assessment plan enabled us to address.

Analyze Perceptual Data

Since district and school reculturing is such a complex and incremental endeavor, perceptions of progress vary greatly; though they vary, these perceptions are important since perceptions affect how we feel and ultimately how we act. While it is true that the first questions leaders should ask is, "What impact are we having on student learning?" this does not mean leaders in professional learning communities are dismissive of the perceptions held by various groups within the organizations. For each of us, our perceptions represent our reality.

A thorough analysis of perception data, such as the result of surveys and interviews, can help district leaders identify misconceptions, as well as areas that need attention. For example, well into the implementation of the PLC process in White River, survey data revealed that a number of teachers felt that the state standards had not been adequately clarified and paced out for the year. This data allowed the district to respond to teacher needs and support their work in teams.

> *A thorough analysis of perception data, such as the result of surveys and interviews, can help district leaders identify misconceptions, as well as areas that need attention.*

Collect Survey and Interview Data

The perceptions of administrators, faculty, and staff regarding the district's progress in implementing professional learning community practices and thus improving student learning should be important elements of a plan to assess the district's progress. White River utilized surveys as one method of determining perceptions of various groups and subgroups regarding *individual components* of the district's efforts to embed professional learning community concepts and practices.

Perception surveys can provide quantifiable data that can be used to track progress in the changing of perceptions over time. For example, in White River, current survey data reveal that many more teachers believe developing and using common formative assessments is important teamwork than when the first surveys were given a few years earlier. Survey data also allow districts to analyze the perceptions of subgroups. For example, principals may have a far more optimistic perception of the implementation of certain PLC practices than the faculty. Finally, surveys allow a district to analyze the implementation of specific components of the professional learning community concept. For example, the White River survey groups questions in such areas as the foundation of mission, vision, values and commitments, and goals; the four critical questions of learning; collaborative teaming; and a focus on results. The entire faculty and staff are encouraged to participate in the survey, and the results allow us to target specific questions for follow-up with specific subgroups in semistructured interviews. The interviews are given *after* an analysis of the survey data. The combination of a broadly administered survey followed by focused, in-depth interviews enables district leaders to better understand how various groups viewed progress in specific areas on the journey to becoming a professional learning community.

While we *strongly* encourage district leaders to develop their own surveys, "A Staff Perceptual Survey on District Progress Toward Becoming a PLC" (page 191) shows the survey instrument White River School District used as an example. Additionally, districts and schools featured at www.allthingsplc.info can share how they have assessed their progress on their journey to becoming a professional learning community.

Analyze Anecdotal Evidence

To understand the importance of anecdotal evidence, we often urge district and school leaders to remember some of the trips they've taken with family or friends—to think of the stories they tell and the highlights they remember. While such memories cannot be measured in a statistical sense, they are nevertheless powerful indicators of our individual and collective experience. For years, anthropologists have cited the important role stories play in not only transmitting culture but also strengthening a culture's core values—especially when stories and anecdotes are linked to public recognition and celebration of faculty and staff. For example, when an administrator publically recognizes a school for its exemplary efforts at providing students with additional time and support within the school day, regardless of the teacher to whom they are assigned, and then tells a story of how a particular student has made remarkable gains, the administrator sends an important signal to everyone within the school district about what values are important.

While a major portion of White River's semistructured interview consisted of questions that were developed as a result of an analysis of the survey data, part of the interview was open-ended and designed to solicit stories and remembrances. We asked questions such as:

- In what ways has working in a professional learning community affected the learning levels of your students?

- How has working in a professional learning community affected you professionally?

While a single comment may not be in and of itself significant, *patterns* of comments can be a strong indicator of perceptions within the district or school.

Analyze Products and Artifacts

Perceptual data gleaned from surveys and interviews provide limited, but useful, information. These data do not, however, monitor the *quality* of work that is being done throughout the district.

In White River, we drilled deeper into quality by examining team products and artifacts against collaboratively developed, predetermined standards of quality. These products and artifacts included such things as team norms, school vision and values and commitments statements, SMART goals, power standards, pacing guides, common formative assessments, and plans to provide students with additional time, support, and enrichment.

Analysis of products and artifacts against predetermined standards enabled us to effectively establish improvement goals not only for the district or schools but also for individual teams. As we discussed in the previous chapter, like students, teams learn and develop at different rates and in different ways. And just as a teacher differentiates instruction to meet individual student needs, a district can differentiate approaches to enhance the quality of the work of district office personnel, individual schools, and individual teams.

What We Have Learned About Assessing District Progress

Developing and utilizing a plan to monitor district progress is of critical importance, yet many districts fail to take this critical step. The goal of any progress assessment plan is to enable district and school leaders to make decisions that will lead to school improvement and student achievement. Our work in assisting districts to monitor their progress on the journey to becoming a professional learning community and thus improving student learning levels has led us to identify the following characteristics of effective district progress-monitoring plans.

Create a Comprehensive Plan

Many districts leaders see the value of assessing their progress from time to time but fail to do so in a systematic, comprehensive, and cyclical manner. While formative assessment of progress occurs throughout the year, we believe it is important to conduct a summative assessment of progress annually. This summative assessment report keeps the school board and everyone within the district fully informed, enables the development of a thorough learning improvement plan, allows for comparisons and a measure of progress, and can be the basis for public recognition and celebration. Additionally, summative data can also be used in the performance appraisal process. For example, in White River, it is common to cite data from the summative report of progress when recognizing the exceptional work of principals or other administrators, and also when identifying an area that warrants attention and improvement. In short, the failure to have a *systematic* plan for assessing progress can lead to conclusions that are incomplete or incorrect and can also contribute to faulty decisions.

Face the Findings

Our work has led us to believe that most district leaders have strongly held views about the progress their district is or is not making. In some districts with which we have worked, leaders assumed, incorrectly, that certain things were being done. Unfortunately, when provided with data that conflict with their views, many leaders have a tendency to either dismiss the data or question the assessment process as inadequate or incomplete. If given credence, *and if the findings are not ignored or simply dismissed*, a comprehensive progress assessment can replace assumptions with facts.

Close Perception Gaps

Perception gaps are not an anomaly; they are the norm.

One of the more interesting things we have learned in our work is that when data from the assessment process are disaggregated, there are often perception differences between and among groups. Perception gaps are not an anomaly; they are the norm. For example, we have found that administrators frequently hold more optimistic views of the progress that is being made than do teachers. It is important, then, to develop the survey and interview instruments in a format that allows for relatively easy disaggregation, and that the information gleaned from the process be used to make decisions and develop initiatives designed to narrow those perception gaps.

Use the Results

The fundamental purpose of any assessment process is informed decision making. Unfortunately, many districts view progress assessment as an end rather than as a means to an end. To put it bluntly, unless the progress assessment process causes district and school leaders to make informed decisions regarding next steps, there is little reason to develop a plan in the first place.

The results of the progress assessment plan must be collaboratively analyzed and summarized in a way that allows district and school leaders to identify successes that can be celebrated as well as target areas that should be improved. The progress-monitoring plan should enable district leaders to set specific improvement goals.

And, importantly, results can play a significant role in shifting district culture from one of compliance—doing things simply because people are directed—to one of commitment—that is, doing things because the results are obvious. Using data is one of the single most powerful ways to influence opinions. District leaders should use every opportunity to publically communicate the incremental results that are being achieved, and a plan to assess progress on the PLC journey can be a valuable tool in this effort.

Keep the Board Involved and Informed

As you go through this process, keep the local board of education involved and informed along the way. It is not enough to infrequently provide a brief update. We have found it helpful for district leaders to share with the board plans for assessing the progress the district is making and plans for keeping the board informed along the way.

While data that are obtained from various assessment methodologies are used primarily for future decision making, they can also be used to inform key constituencies—especially the local board of education. The amount and quality of support a district receives from the board is directly

> *The amount and quality of support a district receives from the board is directly linked to the degree the district ensures the board is fully engaged and informed.*

linked to the degree the district ensures the board is fully engaged and informed. While no particular format is necessarily preferable, the report format used annually in the White River School District can serve as an example (see "Assessing Our PLC Progress," page 199).

In addition to making regularly scheduled formal summative reports to the board, put faces with data and information. For example, in White River, principals, teachers, staff, and students regularly present at board learning meetings to inform and interact with the board regarding progress that is being made within the district. These and similar approaches go a long way in adding meaning and context to data, and assist the board in gaining a deeper and richer understanding of successes that are being achieved as well as next steps that need to be taken.

Inform Parents and the Larger Community

District leaders should use results of the progress assessment plan to inform parents and the larger community of progress schools are making, particularly highlighting improvements in student learning. Every district should have a comprehensive plan for keeping parents and the community informed, and the plan should include periodic success stories gleaned from the progress assessment process. These incremental success stories can go a long way toward developing a shared perception with parents and the community that the school district is moving in a positive direction.

Listen to the Stories

In White River, the power of the stories that were being shared really helped us know whether or not we were changing the culture. The following are just a few of the dozens of stories that have emerged from the White River journey.

- A thirty-year veteran teacher remarked that as she neared retirement, she realized that the past few years had been the best of her career, and as she worked with her collaborative team, she wanted to have everything in place for the teacher who followed her.

- An algebra team leader shared that once a team does the work of a professional learning community over time, that work then becomes the new normal—just how we do things! He observed that team members often forgot what they had to do to get there—and they often forgot to celebrate along the way. "Five years ago," he said, "our conversations were so general. Rather than digging deep into the learning of each kid, skill by skill, on chapter 3, we used to ask, 'Did you teach chapter 3?'"

- A high school principal, the 2011 Washington State principal of the year, when speaking of the importance of thoughtfully selecting team leaders, often tells how, as a football coach, he used to give far more attention to the selection of his assistant coaches than he initially did as a new principal to the selection of team leaders!

As stories such as these began to pop up in White River, we realized we were incrementally impacting the district culture in ways that compounded over time.

Celebrate, Celebrate, Celebrate

While a progress assessment plan is an essential tool for setting improvement goals, it should also be the basis for publically recognizing, honoring, and celebrating the work of individuals and groups—both students and adults. Frequent, meaningful recognition and celebration are important ways for district and school leaders to sustain the improvement process. This is particularly important for districts undertaking the journey to becoming a professional learning community, since the journey is never completed—rather, districts seeking to function as professional learning communities are constantly working to create a culture of continuous improvement. So, the question is this: How do district leaders sustain a process that is never ending? The answer is in the frequent, meaningful, and genuine recognition and appreciation of incremental achievements. It's not enough to always be looking ahead, planning next the next steps. Just like mountain climbers, periodically district leaders must remind faculty and staff to turn around, look back, and celebrate just how far they've come!

Reflections

District leaders must model the behavior that is expected of others. Modeling is one of the critical ways leaders communicate what they value, and one of the most important values that leaders must model is a focus on results—constant attention to the question, How well are we doing? Consider how your district or school assesses its progress on embedding professional learning community practices in order to ensure high levels of learning for all students.

Individually or in teams, reflect on questions such as the following.

1. Has your district or school developed a plan to assess progress related to implementing professional learning community concepts and practices?

2. Have the data gleaned from the plan been disaggregated by various subgroups (administrators, teachers, support staff, and so on)?

3. How have the data been used? Have the findings from the assessment plan been utilized for decision-making purposes? For goal setting?

4. How have the data been shared?

5. Have the findings from the plan been shared with the board of education? With parents and the broader community?

6. Have the findings been used to publically recognize and celebrate individuals and groups for the progress that has been made?

7. What do you think are the most significant things that can be done to improve the way your district or school addresses the question, How well are we doing?

Epilogue

The journey to becoming a professional learning community is never smooth. Reculturing organizations is a difficult, complex, and incremental endeavor. There are inevitably bumps in the road. Bumps provide an obvious platform for the folks in the district who are just waiting to proclaim, "I told you so. I knew this wouldn't work!" Many districts allow these bumps to stall the work, or even worse, immediately jump to implement the latest fad in education.

Hitting a bump doesn't mean the entire initiative is flawed. In every school, every team will struggle at one time or another, and when it does, it will simply need additional time and support. The absolute worst thing that can happen when a team struggles with the work is to be told, "Oh, okay, you don't have to do it." *Stopping is not an option.* In a professional learning community, if a team is struggling with a piece of the work, someone from the district office, a building principal, or another team is called in to provide help and support to the team. Don't give up, and don't wait for teams to become frustrated and impatient. Provide support quickly, so the bump in the road doesn't become a parking lot!

Making sure everyone is happy, while *desirable*, is not the goal. Improving student *learning* levels through the work of collaborative teams is the goal. The real challenge is not avoiding the inevitable bumps, but learning from them! Sometimes we are quick to forget that there were problems with our old methods of doing things. Sometimes, we just need to stop and ask, "How well were our old ways of doing things working for us?" Bumps can actually help district leaders further clarify their work and sharpen their purpose. The fact is, the schools and districts we've worked with got *better* from their bumps and challenges—and continue to do so. Bumps force us to stop, think, reflect, and deploy a new strategy, and what we learn from that experience makes us wiser in the future.

Some teams will want to pick and choose the work they prefer to do. But each PLC practice is connected to the other PLC practices. The efficacy of the PLC concept is dependent on the synergy that is gained through the interaction of various practices that form the framework of a professional learning community.

The teams that get results do *all* of the work of a professional learning community. They identify their power standards. They craft common formative assessments that are aligned with the standards. They come together to score the assessments, and they use the results of those common assessments to drive the additional time, support, and enrichment for their kids. The power of the professional learning community concept is only effective to the degree that the concept is implemented in its entirety.

> *The teams that get results do all *of the work of a professional learning community.*

It's not easy. In our work with schools and districts, we often hear the cry, "This work makes us tired!" Have you ever met a teacher who wasn't tired before winter holidays and ready to get out of school in June? Teachers have always been tired.

But we found there is a new kind of tired when teachers are tired from doing the right work for the right reasons. Teachers in a true professional learning community are tired because the work is collaborative in nature, because it is focused and intentional, and because it makes teachers really think hard about their students and what they are learning. It makes them think about what their data are showing; often they realize, "Wow, I've got to get to that kid!" It is much more rewarding for faculty and staff to be tired for the right reasons—doing significant work that results in improved student learning!

Appendix

From: Janel Keating
To: Faculty and Staff
Subj: Professional Learning Communities as a Way of Thinking

A Way of Thinking: What Does This Mean?

In my September email regarding the research supporting the concepts and practices of professional learning communities, I emphasized that the professional learning community concept is not a program or an initiative, but a way of thinking about consolidating best practices into a rational approach to education. While I think this is an easy concept to grasp, it perhaps is a little more difficult to connect a "way of thinking" to the real day-to-day world of what goes on in schools and classrooms.

Four Principles for Problem Solving

The White River School District is a busy place! Schools, teams, and individual teachers are constantly tackling complex issues to be more effective. As we deal with various issues, it is helpful to keep four operating principles in mind to be not only more effective in our work, but also more efficient.

First, Build a Guiding Coalition

Most of the issues we are tackling are complex, with few simple answers (or even right ones). We are constantly asking ourselves, "Is there a better way?" For example, is there a better way of thinking about homework, scheduling, or grading?

It is virtually impossible for an entire faculty to have effective dialogue, initially, about these kinds of issues. First, there are simply too many people involved—each with his or her own background, experiences, and opinions. So, typically, we end up talking at each other and at best end up averaging opinions. The fact is, a large group is ill-suited for building consensus.

It is usually, but not always, preferable to start with a few staff members who can begin to address the topic or issue in a more business-like and rational approach. The creation of a guiding coalition or leadership team is a critical step in the complex task of leading a school. By beginning with a smaller group, it is easier later to build consensus with the entire faculty.

Building Shared Knowledge

Nowhere is the phrase *a way of thinking* more applicable than with the idea that the first step a group should take, after clearly defining the issues, is to gain shared knowledge. When a school (or team, or group) functions as a professional learning community,

Source: White River School District. Used with permission.

members attempt to answer questions and resolve issues by first building shared knowledge. In other words, members of a learning community learn together. A major cultural shift occurs when a school begins functioning as a professional learning community and moves from averaging opinions about issues to gaining shared knowledge.

The best way to think of gaining shared knowledge is to think of it as seeking out best practices. For example, if we are trying to improve the way we assign or grade homework, we would first seek out best homework practices—practices that are having a positive impact on student learning. This doesn't necessarily mean studying research. Although research findings are an important aspect of gaining shared knowledge, best practices may be found within our own school or in a neighboring school within the district. Best practices may be found in articles or books. Best practices may be found in the classroom next door. Think of it like this: in professional learning communities, teams seek to learn.

A Culture of Experimentation

Of course, simply learning about effective practices will do little to improve a school unless we are willing to try them out, to experiment. A willingness to try new approaches is a significant aspect of thinking in a professional learning community. Simply put, we won't know unless we try. This requires a willingness to move beyond the status quo. However, a word of caution is in order. We must avoid the "Yeah, but . . ." syndrome of obsessing on the flaws in any idea. There will be an obvious downside to any new initiative. If we refuse to try things because they may not be perfect, we'll never try anything. The goal is not to reach perfection, but to be better. The culture of a school that functions as a professional learning community is one of continuous improvement, incrementally, over time. This only happens if we are willing to close the knowing-doing gap and experiment with new ideas.

A Focus on Results

Often people are reluctant to try new ideas because they are fearful that if things aren't better (or get even worse) they will be stuck with them. This is a legitimate concern. In the White River School District, we must make a commitment that when we experiment with new ideas or approaches, we will assess the effectiveness of our changes and be willing to make adjustments or try something else. A failed initiative can be a good thing if it's handled correctly. That is, by thoughtfully analyzing what has happened and why it happened, we can learn many things that will be beneficial in the future.

In analyzing the effectiveness of our efforts, we must ask the right question: How is this initiative affecting student learning and our mission to ensure high levels of learning for all students who attend White River schools? This may seem obvious, but it is very easy to slip into the habit of first asking, "How do we like it?" While we should not be insensitive to our preferences, we must align our focus on results with the essential goals we are trying to accomplish.

An Example

In visiting district schools, I have noticed an increased interest in the issue of grading practices. I think this is a partly a result of the presentations that many of our staff heard at the Professional Learning Communities at Work Institute in Seattle in August. And, of course, Bob Eaker talked of this issue with the elementary and middle school faculty when he was here a few weeks ago.

There are few more topics more emotional than grading and report cards. We all have strong views on the topic. Yet we can all agree it is important and an area in which we could definitely improve our professional practice. The issue is how to think of this issue in a rational and effective way.

Having the entire school faculty address this topic will be problematic at best. There will simply be too many strong opinions. It may prove to be more effective by having a smaller task force or ad hoc group first tackle the issue. The group's charge should be clearly defined, and part of this charge should be first to gain shared knowledge, to learn about best grading practices. (Of course, these will vary depending on grade levels, disciplines, and so on.)

After learning, analyzing, and discussing, the task force should periodically update the faculty on their work, sharing what they are learning, engaging in a deep, professional dialogue, and, most important, listening deeply to faculty concerns and questions. Then the group can recommend to the administration and faculty that the schools try particular changes. It is important to share with the larger group how the effects of the experiment will be monitored and how adjustments, if needed, will be considered.

This way of thinking can prove to be more effective that simply "throwing it open" in a faculty meeting.

Where Do We Go From Here?

As I mentioned earlier, there is much going on within our district. It is exciting and complex (and, yes, difficult) work. But it is worthwhile, and it is making a huge difference. As we approach various issues and topics ranging from grading and homework to scheduling and giving students additional time and support, it will be helpful if we keep in mind that the quality of what we do will be determined, to a great extent, by how we think and how we act. What I have shared in this email is merely one way of thinking about connecting best practices into a rational, logical approach to ensure that we stretch the aspirations and performance levels of all of us within the White River School District—students and adults alike. And, as Martha Stewart would say, "That's a good thing!"

As always, I welcome and value your thoughts, comments, ideas, and suggestions. And, by the way, let me again say thank you for working so hard to make White River a special place for all of us—students, faculty and staff, parents, and our entire community.

From: Janel Keating
To: White River Faculty and Staff
Subj: The Role of Support Staff in a Professional Learning Community

What Does It Mean?

In the White River School District, what is meant by the statement, "The support staff is a critical component of a school or school district that is seeking to function as a professional learning community"?

Each of the words—*professional, learning, community*—is important for a school or school district that is seeking to function as a professional learning community. And each is very important when thinking of the role of the support staff. Obviously, the support staff desires to work as professionals, in a professional atmosphere. Just like other professionals, the support staff should be seeking out and embedding best practices into their daily work.

Also, the support staff has a role to play in helping fulfill the fundamental mission of the White River School District: ensuring high levels of learning for all students. In this regard, we are all support staff. We just have differing roles to play.

But, most important, the support staff is an integral part of our community. The very term *community* denotes inclusiveness, not exclusiveness. Members of the support staff are valued members of our educational community. In many ways, schools are analogous to families, where each member is valued for his or her individuality and unique contributions, but at the same time shares a commonality. In other words, if we really want to be successful, we must realize that the White River School District is more than a collection of "I's." We are a family of "we's."

Why Is This Important?

While a feeling of being valued and included is essential, that is not the only reasons the support staff are viewed as significant members of a professional learning community. In the White River School District, we are committed to the professional learning community concepts regardless of the position we hold—concepts such as collaboration, seeking out best practice, experimentation and continuous improvement, collaborative analysis of the impact of our efforts, and a collective responsibility for results. These principles apply to all of us in each and every aspect of our work.

Source: White River School District. Used with permission.

Within the White River School District, we have made a conscious effort to include support staff in our professional learning community work, both at the individual school level and at the district level.

Summary

For the first time in the history of American public education, we are being called on to educate at high levels all of the students who attend our schools. This is no small challenge. Perhaps there was a time when society and schools were less complex, and the individual teacher with a group of his or her students could be successful. Our challenges today are so complex that success requires the collaborative efforts of *all* of us within the White River School District. We want *everyone* to be valued contributing members of our community, with each of us focused on our fundamental mission of ensuring high levels of learning for all students. At the very heart of the issue is the fact that within our school district we want to make sure all students learn, rather than merely attend. And to accomplish this goal, we need the collective efforts of each member of our family.

Annual Administrative Performance Evaluation: Hidden Valley School District

Name: **Mr. Smith**
Assignment: **Happy Springs Elementary School Principal**
School Year: **2009–2010**

The Hidden Valley School District places a premium on *reflective practice*, the assumption being that everyone—students, administration, faculty, and support staff—can benefit from reflecting on the quality of his or her work. The impact of reflective practice is enhanced when we consider views from others as well. Therefore, the following observations are meant to encourage personal reflection and serve as a framework and impetus for focused improvement.

The Role of the Building Principal

Over thirty years of research has validated the critical role principals play in effective schools. It is unrealistic to think that Hidden Valley can achieve its vision of excellent schools where all students learn at high levels unless building principals demonstrate the highest quality leadership behaviors. While every school and every situation is unique, there are a number of areas of emphasis where Hidden Valley has chosen to be *tight*. While principals must deal with a wide range of complex issues—often at the same time—the areas discussed in this principal evaluation form the framework of expectations for the role of the principal in Hidden Valley.

An Intense and Passionate Focus on Learning

☑ Meets Expectations   ☐ Improvement Needed   ☐ Below Expectations

Since 2006, Hidden Valley has worked to fundamentally change the district culture. Nowhere is this change more important than shifting the district culture from one emphasizing that the correct curriculum was *taught* and that the appropriate content was *covered* to one emphasizing student learning. In this district, this is much more than mere semantics. The standard for the district is simple: what would our work look like *if we really meant it?* Equally important is the question, *Would this be good enough for my own child?*

Source: White River School District. Adapted with permission.

If we really mean it when we say that our purpose is to ensure high levels of learning for all students, then it follows that each principal will lead the effort to clarify *what* we want students to learn, create a process designed to determine *if* students are learning, and provide additional time and support to *enhance* the learning of all students—those who are experiencing difficulty and those who are moving well beyond proficiency. *If we really mean it*, principals will provide leadership in assessing the impact of current policies, practices, and procedures within their building and measure each decision against their probable impact on learning.

Recognizing that principals must provide high-quality leadership for developing a school culture reflective of an intense and passionate focus on learning, the following observations are offered.

Summary Observations

There is clear evidence that shows that Mr. Smith is working to restore a focus on learning at Happy Springs. He has done a terrific job focusing his own efforts and energy and the efforts and energy of his staff on learning. He has established processes and procedures that will enhance learning. These accomplishments serve as evidence that Happy Springs is accomplishing our mission to ensure high levels of learning for all students. Mr. Smith:

- Planned and organized meeting time schedule that explicitly highlights the learning work ahead of the Happy Springs staff; the work has a direct link to the four critical questions of learning and the district and building learning improvement plan.

- Holds monthly team leader meetings focused on learning

- Uses effective written communication

- Ensures fidelity to the Wednesday PLC work

- Developed a master schedule that meets the learning needs of the children

- Established the RTI process and worked to develop protocols and train staff to use protocols in an effort to ensure a productive meeting

- Ensures that results of RTI meetings change practice in the classroom.

- Has PBIS work in progress

- Increased MSTP reading achievement in grades 3, 4, and 5

- Increased MSTP math achievement in grades 3 and 4

- Increased MSTP writing achievement in grade 4

- Increased MSTP science achievement in grade 5

- Joined with staff and elementary colleagues to continue to refine math program; together they worked to link assessment questions to the state standards, clarified what the standards would look like in student work, and scored the assessments together to ensure progress was reported accurately across the district.

- Revisited with staff the key elements of the primary reading program; training was also provided.

- Has begun to work with staff to build shared knowledge and experiment with best practice surrounding feedback, homework, and grading practices

- Supported ongoing training efforts that helped retool his staff in the area of teaching writing

Mr. Smith has given back to his profession by willingly presenting at the Solution Tree–Washington State ASCD–Hidden Valley PLC workshop for the second year.

Next Steps

Attend as many of the staff trainings as possible.

Continue to ensure fidelity to PLC work.

Developing a Collaborative Culture: Emphasizing the Use of Collaborative Teams

☑ Meets Expectations   ☐ Improvement Needed   ☐ Below Expectations

The Hidden Valley School District will not reach its core purpose of achieving high levels of learning for all students if we continue as a culture where teachers work in isolation. Knowing that it is highly improbable that a collaborative culture will simply appear, principals must provide the leadership necessary to create a high-quality collaborative culture that focuses on the critical *questions and practices* associated with improved learning.

A collaborative culture can be reflected in a number of ways, but the most significant is the use of high-performing collaborative teams. Hidden Valley principals must not only organize their schools into collaborative teams, they must lead the effort to ensure that *each team is focusing on the right things*, and that *each team is continually improving*. In the Hidden Valley School District, enhancing the effectiveness of each individual collaborative team is recognized as a key aspect of principalship.

Principals are expected to be contributing members of the district-level administrative team. The administrative team should model the behaviors that are expected of teacher teams. The administrative team should rehearse and practice the work that will be expected of the collaborative teams in their buildings. As a team, principals will share and reflect on the results of their efforts, as well as share suggestions for improvement.

In light of the critical role the principal plays in creating a high-quality collaborative culture and enhancing the effectiveness of collaborative teams to improve learning levels of students, the following observations are offered.

Summary Observation

Notable progress has been made with the collaborative teams at Happy Springs. Teams have identified norms and protocols to guide their work together. Mr. Smith has provided the structure teams need to analyze student achievement data and establish SMART goals that they are working interdependently to achieve. Mr. Smith provided the teams time to do the work and reflect on the results, and he created a venue to share the results with the entire staff. The unit plan work at Happy Springs was the best in the Hidden Valley School District. Mr. Smith did an effective job of giving feedback to each team on its unit plans. The Happy Springs survey data suggest that all teams are focused on the critical questions of learning. (See attachment for additional data and observations.)

Mr. Smith worked with one grade-level team to improve its focus, practices, and procedures to improve learning. He isn't afraid to have the difficult conversation surrounding appropriate pacing and assessment challenges.

Mr. Smith trained his team leaders and played a key role in training team leaders districtwide.

Next Steps

Mr. Smith's challenge at Happy Springs is to get collaborative teams to continue to focus on the work of a learning community. Therefore during the 2010–2011 academic year, attention will continue to be paid to helping individual teams focus on each student skill by skill. Specificity is expected. There's evidence that Mr. Smith is already leading in this direction. I appreciate that he includes me on the emails as he works to hold teams and individuals accountable for the work.

Mr. Smith will need to spend more time with teams that need attention and support.

Mr. Smith will need to redesign the RTI schedule making him available to the grade-level teams on Wednesday morning.

Mr. Smith needs to visit classrooms regularly to observe the work of the team in action and observe the learning.

Teams will continue with an intentional plan to monitor the goals and gather evidence of progress on those goals at regular checkpoints.

Teams will need to continue to adhere to pacing guides to help students achieve the essential standards. Special attention will need to be directed toward the use of the math pacing and assessment binder.

Teams will need to implement SOAR (Student Online Assessment Resource).

Teams will not only write and refine common formative assessments, but will also continue to use the district protocols to analyze the results and to identify students who need additional time and support to master the standards. Analyzing the results of frequent, timely, common formative assessments will enhance the effectiveness of intervention time.

Teams will continue the unit planning process to a guaranteed and viable curriculum for our Hidden Valley kids. Mr. Smith will be held responsible for evidence linked to that process.

Teams will continue to implement "grading for learning" practices and share the effect on improving student learning. Mr. Smith will monitor that these researched practices are being used in the classrooms and reflected in communication with parents.

Teams will begin articulation work with the middle school in the areas of math and writing.

Teams will need to be provided time to build shared knowledge regarding effective reading practices and how those practices can influence Happy Springs reading data.

One key to Mr. Smith's success in his position as Happy Springs principal—ensuring high levels of learning for all students—depends on the leadership capacity of the team leaders in each school. Team leaders will be expected to enhance the capacity of their team to work *interdependently* to achieve *common* goals for which team members hold themselves *mutually accountable*. Team leaders are responsible for functions such as leading the team in preparing and utilizing team norms, planning agendas, chairing meetings, serving as a direct communications link between the administration and the faculty, leading the work of teams in analyzing and improving student learning data, seeking out and experimenting with best practices, leading the collaborative development and attainment of learning improvement goals, and identifying and communicating professional development needs. *Team leaders must work continually to enhance the effectiveness of their teams by ensuring that their teams focus on the critical questions and practices associated with improving student learning in a style that is reflective of the highest quality.*

A Focus on Results

☑ Meets Expectations   ☐ Improvement Needed   ☐ Below Expectations

Our efforts to change the Hidden Valley culture will be in vain unless we can demonstrate results. For us, that means asking, *"Are more students learning more, and how do we know?"* Much as collaborative teams of teachers are asked to reflect on the effectiveness of their own professional practice, so are building principals. What evidence do we have that we are making a positive difference in the learning levels of students? In Hidden Valley, there is an emphasis on *patterns of data*—both quantitative and qualitative. Both norm-referenced and criterion-referenced data are analyzed, and data are disaggregated in specific subgroups.

Is there evidence that students are achieving at higher levels over time? Which students, and in what subject areas? Are students making better grades? Which students are struggling? Are fewer students failing? How are students performing on various standardized tests such as the SAT and AP exams? How are our students doing on the Washington Assessment of Student Learning/MSP? Recognizing that data only has meaning when viewed in comparison to others, how do our students perform in relation to others? Basically, what evidence do we have that more students are learning more?

Realizing the importance of setting high-quality learning goals, each principal is expected to lead in the development, implementation and monitoring of a learning improvement plan. The learning improvement plan is Hidden Valley's way of organizing for learning improvement. Principals are expected to develop a high-quality learning improvement plan and to provide evidence of progress toward attaining each SMART goal within the plan.

Realizing the central importance of evidence of student learning and the usefulness of a learning improvement plan for setting learning improvement goals, the following observations are made.

Summary Observations

There is evidence of a learning "trophy case" at Happy Springs. There are tremendous displays of student work in the hallways. The standards are posted, and visitors often see the rubrics posted as well.

Mr. Smith established an effective unit reflection process with his staff at the team and building level.

Mr. Smith worked with the district office to redesign the "analyzing the data" tool.

Mr. Smith worked to refine intervention time at Happy Springs. He established the RTI process and the protocols that would guide conversation of the RTI teams. Several Tier 2 and 3 interventions are now in place.

Mr. Smith led the way for his principal colleagues to share data at the principal data team meetings.

Next Steps

Mr. Smith will:

- Continue to work with team leaders to monitor the team goals on a timely basis
- Continue unit reflection process at team and building level
- Continue to work with administration team and BLC to monitor the results of the Tier 2 and 3 intervention classes
- Work with his administration team to enhance learning opportunities for students already meeting the standard
- Build in celebrations for the students and staff

Leadership in the Nonacademic Areas

☑ Meets Expectations ☐ Improvement Needed ☐ Below Expectations

While ensuring high levels of learning for all students is the core mission of the Hidden Valley School District, there are other areas of schooling that cannot go unattended. Organizing and managing the day-to-day tasks associated with schooling is a real challenge for principals. It is unreasonable to think that principals can effectively lead schools to higher levels of learning if the nonacademic areas are not done well. Also, we cannot assume that student learning will automatically increase just because a principal does an excellent job at managing the day-to-day activities. Academic and nonacademic areas go hand in hand, with high-quality leadership expected in both areas—not one area at the expense of another.

This area consists of organizational and management skills such as planning, monitoring, and timely follow-through. Principals are expected to develop, implement, and monitor plans for excellent school, parent, and community relations, as well as a host of activities within the school. Principals are expected to actively support and implement district priorities and goals.

There is also the issue of how well principals handle the unexpected and unplanned. Principals manage the physical plant, ensuring that the facilities and grounds are safe, clean, secure, and attractive, always asking, "Would this be good enough for my own child?" To this end, the following observations are provided.

Summary Observations

Mr. Smith is a team player and professional in every way. He truly worked side by side with the district office as we work to improve learning in Hidden Valley. He is not afraid to ask difficult questions as he works to try to understand some of the district office decisions. I appreciate his questions and his general probing nature. He has learned that being patient can benefit his school.

Mr. Smith has developed strong relationships with all members of the Admin Council. He finds value and learns from his elementary, middle level, and high school colleagues. Mr. Smith is part of a terrific group of leaders who are models for working together to take collective responsibility for the learning of all kids in the district.

Mr. Smith genuinely cares about the students and families in Hidden Valley. Mr. Smith does a terrific job representing the Hidden Valley School District at every event. Increasingly he is being called on to share his expertise outside the district.

In short, Mr. Smith is a wonderful person. We all enjoy working with him.

Leadership and Leading Cultural Change

☑ Meets Expectations   ☐ Improvement Needed   ☐ Below Expectations

No one would deny that the role of the building principal is a difficult and complex challenge. Few would deny, either, that the leadership capacity of principals is the driving force behind highly effective schools—especially those striving to function as professional learning communities. While the term *leadership* means different things to different people, in Hidden Valley, the measure is this: *how well is the principal leading the school in its efforts to function as a professional learning community in order to positively impact student learning?*

Although there is not a single set of behaviors that form a *checklist* of effective leadership behaviors, principals in Hidden Valley should be modeling a *simultaneous loose-tight* approach to changing school culture. While everyone within the school is expected to demonstrate improvement, each person is also entitled to support from the administrative team. Principals must model *reciprocal accountability* and *servant leadership*.

To what degree is the principal modeling *seeking out best practice* and increasing his or her own knowledge base about leadership and organizational management to more effectively lead others? Is the principal enhancing the leadership capacity of others, especially collaborative teams? If leaders are ultimately to be effective, they must *touch the emotions*; how well does the principal motivate and inspire? Does the principal have the skills to effectively confront behavior that is incongruent with the mission, vision, and shared commitments of the school and school district, while at the same time frequently and publically recognizing the success of individuals and groups as they reflect the very best of the district's commitment to ensuring high levels of learning in a collaborative culture?

Since the leadership capacity of principals is of such critical importance, the following observations are made.

Summary Observations

Mr. Smith has many characteristics of what Jim Collins refers to as a Level 5 leader. He is just the right mix of personal humility and professional will. He is first to look out the window to attribute success to factors other than himself. He is also willing to look in the mirror and take full responsibility when things don't go just as planned. Mr. Smith is working to develop and recognize those Level 5 leaders at Happy Springs.

Next Steps

Mr. Smith needs to continue to spend time building relationships with his staff and parent community. These relationships will benefit Mr. Smith and the students at Happy Springs.

The administrator's signature assures that he or she has read and discussed the evaluation with the evaluator. It does not necessarily signify agreement with the evaluation.

Administrator's Signature	Evaluator's Signature
Date	Date

From: Janel Keating
To: Faculty and Staff
Subj: Collaborative Teams in a Professional Learning Community

What Does the Term *Collaborative Team* Mean?

A number of important cultural shifts must occur if schools (or districts) are to successfully move from a more traditional culture to one that is reflective of a professional learning community. The most basic of these is a shift from a culture of teacher isolation that characterizes many schools to a collaborative culture where teachers work together as part of a collaborative team. In a professional learning community, teachers are contributing members of a team that is working interdependently to achieve common goals that are designed to improve their professional practice and student learning. There are some key words in the previous sentence that provide an intellectual framework for thinking about collaborative teams in schools that function as true professional learning communities—words such as *contributing, interdependently, common, improve,* and *learning*. Unless attention is paid to each of these key words, we won't have collaborative teams in the White River School District; we'll simply have groups of teachers who are already stressed and overworked doing even more busywork.

In a professional learning community, the focus is not simply on whether we have organized our schools into high-performing teams, but rather what the teams do. So, what should be the focus of a team's work? In a professional learning community, teams focus on the major questions and issues that have the biggest impact on student learning. For example, they are constantly clarifying the essential outcomes that students are expected to learn in every subject, grade, or course, and constantly improving the alignment with state and district curriculum standards. They set curriculum and learning priorities and collaborate about the pacing of the curriculum. Collaborative teams write periodic formative assessments designed to monitor the learning of subgroups and individual students on a timely basis, and they collaboratively analyze the results of these assessments and set learning improvement goals. Teams collaboratively analyze and assess the quality of student work and develop rubrics that define the level of quality that students should achieve. They engage in study about such important issues as best practices in grading, feedback, homework, and so on. And they are constantly seeking ways to provide additional time and support for students who are having difficulty with their learning, as well as publically celebrating and stretching the performance levels of

Source: White River School District. Used with permission.

students who are learning. But most importantly, they accept the *collective* responsibility for ensuring that their students are learning at high levels.

Also, in a collaborative team culture, the teachers not only provide support for students, they learn from and support each other. Let's face it, being a teacher can be a very lonely, private, and stressful profession if teachers are left on their own to fend for themselves. In a professional learning community, teams of teachers work together to deal with issues and solve problems, making success seem more doable. Ultimately, the use of collaborative teams provides teachers with a culture of understanding, caring, and support.

One of the first things high-performing teams do is collaboratively write explicit norms to guide their work in the process of building the capacity to work effectively as a collaborative team. The process of developing these norms or guidelines helps clarify how the team will function, expectations, and expected behaviors. Norms also help team members be accountable. There will be that time when someone will fail to honor the norms that have been agreed upon. Referring back to the norms can help the members of the team reflect on what the group values and stands for, to bring the group back into focus.

In short, collaborative teams of teachers are the heart and soul of a school that functions as a professional learning community.

Why Is This So Important?

Most 21st century organizations look very different from the organizations most of us grew up with and are familiar with. The old hierarchical, top-down organizational structure has given way to a much flatter organization where the emphasis is on the use of high-performing collaborative teams. The power of teams is illustrated in Berry and Seltman's (2008) *Management Lessons From the Mayo Clinic: Inside One of the World's Most Admired Service Organizations*. In describing the culture and values of the Mayo Clinic, they observe:

> *Collaboration, cooperation, and coordination are the three dynamics supporting the practice of team medicine at Mayo Clinic. These dynamics drive the delivery of personalized care for patients, although staff members care for thousands of patients each day. Individual staff members—from physician to custodian—become active team players to serve patients' needs because treating complex illnesses requires the diverse expertise available from all personnel and the supporting infrastructure. To work at Mayo is to be on the team. (Berry & Seltman, 2008, p. 65)*

It is interesting that despite wave after wave of "reforms" in public education, the task of teaching continues, in most schools, to fall upon a single individual teacher standing alone before a group of students, working in isolation. Teachers report that one of their greatest sources of dissatisfaction is their perception that they scarcely know their colleagues and have little time to discuss issues related to curriculum and instruction. The isolation of teachers is one of the most formidable roadblocks to ensuring that students learn at high levels and that teachers feel a sense of community, caring, support, and professionalism.

There is absolutely no research to support the proposition that the best way to significantly improve schools is to have teachers working alone, by themselves. Yet there is overwhelming research to support the use of high-performing collaborative teams. Creating a collaborative environment has been described by Eastwood and Seashore Louis (1992) as the single most important factor for successful school improvement initiatives and the first order of business for those seeking to improve schools.

However, a word of caution is in order. Some schools mistake the term *collaboration* with *congeniality*. While getting along is a worthy goal, this is not what the team concept is about. Rather, the use of high-performing teams is designed to be a systematic process in which teachers work together, interdependently, to analyze and improve their own professional practices and improve the learning levels of students. The research supporting the practice of arranging personnel into teams has been identified as an important factor linked to school improvement.

An interesting question is this: So, are we a profession? Bob Eaker and the DuFours have consistently written in their books on professional learning communities of the need for schools to seek out best practices, pointing out that basing what we do on proven practice is a distinguishing characteristic of a profession. With the lack of any credible evidence supporting a culture of teacher isolation and a vast amount of research supporting the use of collaborative teams, how can we as a profession continue to utilize school structures that not only allow but, in many cases, support teacher isolation?

In fact, isn't it ultimately just a question of common sense? Perhaps Handy put it best when he wrote, "People who collaborate learn from each other and create synergy. That is why learning organizations are made up of teams that share a common purpose. Organizations need togetherness to get things done and to encourage the exploration essential to improvement" (Handy, 1995, p. 47).

From: Janel Keating
To: Faculty and Staff
Subj: How Will We Respond When Students Experience Difficulty With Their Learning?

A focus on learning requires attention to a critical question: How will we respond when students experience difficulty with their learning? Virtually every educator will acknowledge the fact that students (and adults for that matter) learn at different rates and in different ways. Yet in more traditional models of schooling, students are expected to achieve at similar levels at roughly the same time. Professional learning communities address this critical issue by developing a systematic series of interventions to ensure students receive additional time and support when they experience difficulty in their learning. DuFour, DuFour, Eaker, and Many (2010) are emphatic on this point noting, "It is disingenuous for any school to claim its purpose is to help all students learn at high levels and then fail to create a system of interventions to give struggling learners additional time and support for learning" (p. 78).

What do these plans look like in the real world of public schools? They vary from school to school, but to be effective, DuFour, DuFour, Eaker, and Many (2010) urge educators to make sure the plan is *systematic*—a written, schoolwide plan that guarantees students receive needed time and support within the regular school day, regardless of who their teacher may be. And, the plan should ensure *timely* interventions for students at the first indication they are experiencing difficulty. Most important, the plan should *direct* rather than invite students to take advantage of the support plan.

Beginning the Journey: The Glacier Middle School Example

While every school in the White River School District is working to collaboratively develop effective plans to provide additional time and support for students who are experiencing difficulty with their learning, the approach of Glacier Middle School serves as an example of how the process of developing effective plans can be accomplished.

Gaining Shared Knowledge

The faculty and staff of Glacier knew that in order to develop an effective plan they would need a smaller working group (a guiding coalition) to seek out best practice. Initially, two resources proved to be very help for getting started. The first, *Visible Learning* by John Hattie (2009), provided a sound research base for providing additional time, support, practice, and specific feedback. The second, *Raising the Bar and Closing the Gap*, by Richard and Becky DuFour, Robert Eaker, and Gayle Karhanek (2010) provided

---

Source: White River School District. Used with permission.

specific examples from schools that had made significant gains in student achievement through the development of a pyramid of interventions.

These examples proved to be particularly significant for the work at Glacier. The educators at Glacier found the case that DuFour, DuFour, Eaker, and Karhanek (2010) put forth to be compelling. They argue that

> *traditionally the response to the question [of how we will respond when students don't learn] has been left to the discretion of individual teachers, leading to a kind of educational lottery for students. We continue to argue that this individualistic and random approach is neither effective nor equitable. We insist that a school committed to helping all students learn at high levels should provide a multilayered collective response that guarantees all students who struggle with receive additional time and support for learning. (p. 1)*

Seeking Out Best Practice

Rather than merely average opinions about how they might provide help to students who were struggling, the faculty and staff decided to seek out schools that had successfully implemented a pyramid of interventions. One of the reasons *Raising the Bar and Closing the Gap* proved to be such a valuable resource is that it contains examples of effective intervention practices from thirty-eight schools from across the United States. One particular school, Lakeridge Junior High School in Orem, Utah, seemed to be a school that could serve as an example for Glacier. After reading about the success that Lakeridge had achieved, the principals of Glacier visited Lakeridge, realizing that even though they might learn a lot, the practices would need to be adapted into Glacier's own unique culture. But they also knew they needed to get started, then they could get better.

Collaboratively Developing a Plan

The fact is, if people care enough about something, they will develop a plan to make sure it happens. Upon return from Utah, the faculty and staff at Glacier began to put together the first pieces of their plan for additional time and support. And even though the plan is now complete, they realize this is simply the first step. They are committed to monitoring the plan and adjusting it along the way. The bottom line for the faculty and staff at Glacier is this—are more kids learning more? What's working and what's not?

Where Do We Go From Here?

At the fall administrative retreat, much discussion among district administrators centered on the need to "drill deeper," focusing on the learning of individual students, kid by kid, skill by skill, and then providing each student appropriate and effective additional time, support, and enrichment. The work at Glacier Middle School is but one example of the work that is being done throughout the district. The Glacier plan [which was attached to the email] is simply the first in a series of emails from me that will feature the intervention plans from each school.

One thing that is very important for you to know is that I know the work across the district in White River is affecting the lives of our children. For that, we should all be proud of being a part of this district and all the great things that are happening.

SAMPLE EMAIL

From: Janel Keating
To: Administrators, Faculty, and Staff
Subj: Why Data Meetings?

There is virtually unanimous agreement among researchers and practitioners regarding the power of formative assessments to positively impact student learning. However, the power of common formative assessments doesn't lie in the assessments, but rather in how the assessments are used. Although individual teachers can benefit from the use of formative assessments to monitor the learning of their students, the impact of formative assessments is greatly enhanced when *teacher teams* collaboratively analyze student learning data, student by student, skill by skill.

If student achievement within classrooms can be impacted by school teams engaging in the collaborative analysis of student learning data, isn't it a logical extension that achievement across a school district can be impacted by districtwide collaborative analysis of student learning data? Equally important, shouldn't district meetings model the work that is expected of others? After all, if we are expecting faculty and staff in individual schools to develop a culture in which they feel comfortable sharing and analyzing student learning data within their teams, should we not work to create the same kind of culture districtwide? We know that one of the most powerful leadership behaviors is simply this: modeling the behavior we expect of others.

In short, we have districtwide data meetings for a number of reasons. We use them to ensure we are crystal clear about what is essential for our students in White River to learn, to collaboratively address the question, Are the students learning, and what are their areas of strength and weakness? We have data meetings to increase specificity and precision regarding providing additional time, support, and enrichment, and to reflect, share, and learn from each other regarding our professional practices—especially instructional practices. And we have them to practice and rehearse the work that will be expected of our teacher teams in each building. In other words, we have data meetings in order to model the work of a professional learning community!

In the White River School District, we are working to create a *culture of formative assessment*, ranging from students assessing their own learning and setting improvement goals, to teacher teams within each school collaboratively analyzing student learning (student by student, skill by skill), to districtwide data meetings in which principals and teachers collaboratively share and analyze student learning data and make plans for continuous improvement to impact every school, every team, every classroom, every student!

Source: White River School District. Used with permission.

Protocols for Data Meetings

1. We will report data tied to the yearlong plan for writing and the end of unit/chapter math assessments. Principals will work with the Deputy Superintendent to set the data meeting dates.

2. Data will be shared at school data meetings prior to being shared at district data meetings.

3. We will use the TACA (Team Analyzing Common Assessment) form as the reporting template. Summative assessment data are sent to the district office. Preassessment and formative assessment data provide information for the use of teachers and teams.

4. Principals will be assigned to present the data on one grade level or content area across the district. A teacher or team from that grade level or content area will present with the principal.

5. District office staff, principals, assistant principals, teachers, WREA (White River Education Association) representation, and DLIP (District Learning Improvement Plan) parents and board members will be invited to attend district data meetings.

6. At each data meeting, strengths in student learning will be identified as well as areas of concern. Ideas for improvement will be generated, discussed, and utilized for decision making and planning.

From: Janel Keating and Bob Eaker
To: Faculty and Staff
Subj: Additional Time and Support for Adults in a Professional Learning Community

We were recently asked if the concept of providing students additional time and support when they experience difficulty also applies to the adults in a school district. Virtually everyone agrees that students learn at different rates and in different ways. So, the idea that some students will need additional time and support strikes a chord with most educators. As one teacher put it, "It just makes sense." But what about adults? Do the same principles apply?

We think the answer is an emphatic yes. In fact, the same principle applies not only to individuals, but to groups of adults as well. Think of it like this—the school is really just a bigger classroom—a classroom of adults. The principal and the district office support staff are the teachers in this bigger classroom, providing additional time and support for those who need it. (Additionally, these teachers are enhancing the learning of those who do get it and are publically celebrating their accomplishments.)

If a school district is passionately and sincerely committed to the notion of improving the learning of all students, it is highly unlikely that each school within the district will progress at the same rate or in the same way. Each school will experience difficulty at one time or another, and when it does, the district office staff should work with the school personnel to develop a plan for additional time and support. And just like for students, the plan should be timely, systematic, and directional.

The same is true for collaborative teams within a school. When a school is organized into collaborative teams, it is unrealistic to think that each team is going to develop, mature, and perform at the same rate and in the same way. Certainly, some teams are going to need more attention, time, and support than others.

For some schools and districts, the notion of ensuring high levels of learning for all is a lofty goal but one that is difficult to achieve. Here's a suggestion: think about breaking it down and focusing on one team at a time.

It becomes doable when, for example, the science department—a department that has already aligned curriculum and written its common assessments—is asked to assist the English teachers as they begin the process of writing common assessments. Perhaps there is a third-grade team in one building that has improved student learning by collaboratively analyzing student work. Wouldn't it be helpful to have this team share its work with other teams within the district? Best practices come alive when they are modeled

Source: White River School District. Used with permission.

and shared by respected teachers. This is only one way of providing teams additional time and support. And it's also a way to improve student learning.

Successful schooling is a difficult and complex endeavor, and everyone needs additional time and support from time to time. But time and support must be tailored to fit each circumstance, since adults, like students, learn in different ways. Think of it as intentionally creating a roadmap—first making sure everyone knows where we are going and why; second, identifying specific steps needed to reach the destination (benchmarks along the way); then providing additional time and support to ensure everyone arrives. Perhaps everyone will not take the same route to the destination or even arrive at the same time, but with frequent monitoring, feedback, and effective time and support, everyone can get to where he or she should be.

We think this is an important aspect of successfully reculturing districts and schools into professional learning communities. What have been your experiences? We invite you to share your thoughts, ideas, and experiences about this important and timely topic.

Professional Learning Communities and the Professional Life of Teachers

In Wisconsin a few years ago, the staff of the National Commission on Teaching and America's Future hosted an invitational meeting at Wingspread, the famed and historical conference center. (The conference center was designed by Frank Lloyd Wright as the family home of H. F. Johnson, founder of the Johnson Wax company.) The commission had been formed in 1994 with Governor James Hunt Jr. of North Carolina serving as the commission's chair. Under the guidance of its executive director, Linda Darling-Hammond of Columbia University, the commission made significant contributions to the improvement of teaching quality, most notably the commission's call for goals and incentives for National Board Certification in every state and school district.

The purpose of the Wingspread meeting was to address a related and significant issue—the quality of the *professional* life of teachers. At the opening session, commission staff members reported that although the quality of new teachers entering the profession had improved dramatically, the number of teachers leaving the profession after five years exceeded the number of high-quality teachers who were entering.

Hope in an Age of Uncertainty

To borrow from Charles Dickens, these are perhaps the best of times and the worst of times for America's teachers. One thing is for sure: it is a time of uncertainty. Teachers are being asked, in fact *required*, to educate at high levels every student who attends school. Since the passing of No Child Left Behind, schools are required to demonstrate that students in all designated demographic subgroups have reached a level of proficiency.

Never before have schools been directed to ensure that *all* students learn at high levels, regardless of socioeconomic or family factors, language difficulties, or ability. As unbelievable as it may seem, until recently it was simply accepted that by its very nature, schooling was a process of sorting and selecting, with the cream eventually rising to the top. Even Thomas Jefferson, who asserted that general education was critical to the vitality of the new republic, proposed a system of education for Virginia designed to ensure that only twenty boys of "best genius" in the state would be "raked from the rubbish annually" to receive up to ten years of schooling at the public expense, and that only half of those would ultimately be admitted to the university each year (Jefferson,

1782). While few would argue with the premise that it is certainly desirable to have all students learn at high levels, accomplishing this worthwhile goal is indeed difficult. In this climate of mandates, accountability, and public scrutiny, many teachers become discouraged and simply succumb to despair. The issue isn't so much a matter of getting highly qualified teachers into the profession. The more complex issue is how to keep them.

The Wingspread meeting was significant because the staff of the National Commission on Teaching and America's Future concluded that schools functioning as true professional learning communities offered the best hope for improving the professional life of teachers and that reculturing schools to reflect the practices inherent in the professional learning community framework offered a ray of hope for keeping good teachers in the profession.

The Professional Life of Teachers in a Professional Learning Community

The commission staff had it right. Schools that function as professional learning communities can indeed be havens of hope for teachers caught in a rather heartless system. How is that? Just how do professional learning communities contribute to the quality of teachers' professional work life?

First, professional learning communities are based on the belief that no program, no curriculum, no technology—and certainly no mandate—will be sufficient to meet the challenge of educating all students at high levels, no matter how hard we try. Teachers will remain the most important resource in the battle for high-quality learning for all students. Thus, professional learning communities are structured to create the conditions in which teachers can continue to grow and learn as professionals (DuFour, DuFour, Eaker, & Many, 2006).

Second, the very role of the teacher is viewed differently in a school that functions as a professional learning community. In traditional schools, administrators are viewed as holding positions of leadership, and teachers are viewed more or less as holding positions of implementation. Professional learning communities break from this traditional norm and view teachers as the key transformational leaders in a school district. After all, who is in the best position to enable students to believe they can do things they have never done before—the principle characteristic of a transformational leader?

Third, professional learning communities focus on not only student learning but adult learning as well. This focus on adult learning characterizes a culture in which teachers become more skillful in their profession. Not only do professional learning communities foster conditions in which teachers get better, teachers are constantly reviewing evidence of their success. Thus, teachers *know* they are effective because they constantly review *evidence* of student learning. This speaks right to the heart of being a professional—the desire to feel successful and take pride in one's work and accomplishments.

The word *community* is especially powerful within the context of a professional learning community. The desire to belong, to be part of a successful endeavor, is an innate human desire. Professional learning communities break down the traditional barriers of isolation and loneliness. Professional learning communities are places of mutual support, respect, and interdependence—places that make the seemingly impossible task of educating all students at high levels doable. The goal of high levels of learning for all students often seems unattainable if one has to work alone in the complex world of a classroom—frequently, for an entire career! On the other hand, professional learning communities create a well-defined structure of support, with colleagues to turn to for support, advice, help, and encouragement.

Last, schools that function as professional learning communities provide a culture of hope. DuFour, DuFour, Eaker, & Many (2006, p. 203) note that

> *professional learning communities set out to restore and increase the passion of teachers by not only reminding them of the moral purpose of their work, but also by creating the conditions that allow them to do that work successfully. The focus is on making a positive difference in the lives of kids rather than on raising test scores. . . . They make heroes of staff members by weaving a never-ending story of committed people who touch both the minds and hearts of their students.*

Think about it: teachers are the very heart and soul of a school that effectively functions as a professional learning community, and as a professional learning community, the quality of the professional life of teachers is greatly enhanced. The good news is that we have the capacity to create such schools right now! And if not now, *when*? And if not us, *who*?

A Staff Perceptual Survey on District Progress Toward Becoming a PLC

		Strongly Agree	Agree	Disagree	Strongly Disagree	N/A
1	Activities have been conducted for the purpose of clarifying what a PLC is and how a PLC works.					
2	I have a good understanding of PLC.					
3	Districtwide activities and processes have been employed to develop a common language about PLC concepts and practices.					
4	The mission of high levels of learning for all students has been clearly articulated by the district and my building.					
5	I believe the learning mission has become embedded in the district's culture.					
6	The staff has collaboratively developed a vision statement that explicitly describes the school we seek to become.					
7	The vision statement is explicit and detailed.					

Source: White River School District. Adapted from Eaker, DuFour, & DuFour, 2002. Used with permission.

page 1 of 8

		Strongly Agree	Agree	Disagree	Strongly Disagree	N/A
8	The vision statement is based on a collaborative effort to develop a shared knowledge about effective schooling practices.					
9	The work of our grade-level or department team supports the vision of the school we want to become.					
10	The staff collaboratively identified core values and commitments that would be necessary to fulfill the vision statement.					
11	The values and commitments statements have been communicated.					
12	High-priority goals have been collaboratively identified.					
13	There is a plan for monitoring the goals.					
14	The goals are written as measurable performance standards.					
15	Procedures and policies have been reviewed in light of their impact on learning.					
16	Decisions are made based on their impact on learning.					
17	Collaboration is embedded into the routine practices of the district and school.					

		Strongly Agree	Agree	Disagree	Strongly Disagree	N/A
18	Teams have identified team norms and protocols to guide us in working together.					
19	We have analyzed student achievement data and have established SMART goals that we are working interdependently to achieve.					
20	Teams focus on the critical questions of learning:					
	What do we expect students to learn?					
	How will we know if they have learned it?					
	How will we, as a school, respond when students experience difficulty in learning?					
	How will we respond when students exceed the standards?					
21	Teams engage in an ongoing search for best instructional practices through collaborative research and dialogue, analyzing student work and observing the "teacher next door."					
22	Each member of my collaborative team is clear on the state grade-level expectations (GLE) for each grade level or course.					

Every School, Every Team, Every Classroom © 2012 Solution Tree Press • solution-tree.com
Visit **go.solution-tree.com/plcbooks** to download this page.

		Strongly Agree	Agree	Disagree	Strongly Disagree	N/A
23	The grade-level expectations drive the work of my collaborative team.					
24	Grade-level teams across the district have identified the big ideas and grade-level expectations, unit by unit.					
25	Team members have agreed on how to best sequence the content of the course or unit and have established pacing guides to help students achieve the intended essential standards.					
26	Teams have identified the prerequisite knowledge and skills students need in order to master the GLE/power standards of our courses and their units.					
27	Teams have identified strategies and created common assessments to determine whether students have the prerequisite knowledge and skills.					
28	Teams have developed strategies for additional time and support to assist students in acquiring prerequisite knowledge and skills when they are lacking in those areas.					

Every School, Every Team, Every Classroom © 2012 Solution Tree Press • solution-tree.com
Visit **go.solution-tree.com/plcbooks** to download this page.

		Strongly Agree	Agree	Disagree	Strongly Disagree	N/A
29	Teams have developed frequent common formative assessments that help us to monitor each student's mastery of essential standards.					
30	Teams have established the proficiency standard we want each student to achieve on each skill and concept examined with our common assessments.					
31	Teams have agreed on the criteria used in judging the quality of student work related to the learning of each course subject.					
32	Teams practice applying those criteria to ensure consistency.					
33	Students know the criteria and rubrics we will use in judging the quality of their work and have been provided with examples.					
34	Teams use the results of common assessments, program assessments, and district assessments to identify students who need additional time and support to master grade-level expectations/ power standards.					

		Strongly Agree	Agree	Disagree	Strongly Disagree	N/A
35	A schoolwide written plan has been developed to ensure that students receive additional time and support when they experience difficulty in mastering essential standards.					
36	The plan to provide students additional time and support is a systematic, schoolwide plan that does not rely on the discretion of individual teachers.					
37	Students who experience difficulty in their learning receive timely intervention by the classroom teacher.					
38	The plan directs students to receive additional time and support rather than inviting them to do so.					
39	A plan has been developed to ensure students receive enrichment and extension in their learning when they demonstrate proficiency.					
40	Student learning data as well as student work are analyzed to identify professional development needs.					
41	Staff have been provided training, support, and resources to enable them to implement PLC concepts and best practices.					

		Strongly Agree	Agree	Disagree	Strongly Disagree	N/A
42	Staff have been given opportunities to read, discuss, and understand current research on assessment, grading, and reporting practices.					
43	Staff have begun changing assessment, grading, and reporting practices to align with current research, and they have evaluated these changes in relation to improving student learning.					
44	Staff development is linked to improving student learning.					
45	Staff development that is based on district, team, and individual goals is targeted on the work in the classroom.					
46	SMART goals have been established by grade-level or department teacher teams.					
47	Grade-level and department team goals on the learning improvement plan are aligned with the school learning improvement plan goals.					
48	School improvement plan goals are aligned with district improvement goals.					

page 7 of 8

		Strongly Agree	Agree	Disagree	Strongly Disagree	N/A
49	Team members receive frequent and timely data feedback evaluating the level of their effectiveness compared to other members of their team.					
50	There is frequent and public recognition and celebration for improvement in student learning.					
51	Plans have been implemented for frequent and public student recognition and celebration of improvement.					
52	Opportunities to come together as cross-district teams (PLC time, extended staff meetings, and districtwide trainings) have improved instruction and assessment practices in my classroom.					
53	The CASL (collaborative analysis of student learning) process provides information on progress and drives changes that improve student learning in the classroom.					
54	Grade-level and department teams take collective responsibility for the learning of all students.					

Assessing Our PLC Progress: Annual Report to the White River Board of Education

Janel Keating, Deputy Superintendent
for Teaching and Learning

INTRODUCTION: THE JOURNEY TO BECOMING A PROFESSIONAL LEARNING COMMUNITY

The White River School District has clearly articulated a mission of ensuring high levels of learning for all students. It has made the commitment to embed *best practices* using the professional learning community framework throughout the district in order to achieve this goal. The journey to becoming a professional learning community is just that—a journey, *not* a destination. Further, the journey is difficult, complex, and incremental—and one that affects *every* aspect of school culture.

There is much to celebrate when reflecting on the successes of students and adults within the district. However, legitimate questions need to be addressed at this stage of our journey: How well are we doing? Where are we? Are more students learning at higher levels as a result of our efforts? What should be our next steps?

While there is no one right way to become a professional learning community, there are definite stops one must make along the way. And just like any successful journey, the White River School District's journey to become a professional learning community requires that we periodically stop and check where we are and determine our next steps.

If we are to model professional learning community practices, we must have a *plan* in place to periodically assess our progress. This plan to assess our progress should not be a one-time event, but rather a process that serves at least four important purposes, over an extended period of time.

1. The plan must enable us to determine our current reality. We should be able to periodically take a snapshot of where we are on our journey.

2. The purpose of the plan must be clear—to enable us to make wise decisions as to our next steps—making sure we are heading in the right direction, with the next stop clearly focused in everyone's mind.

3. The plan to assess our progress on the PLC journey must model the PLC practices we expect of others. After all, frequent monitoring of results is a critical component of the professional learning community framework. If we expect teams of teachers and staff to develop a plan that frequently and

---

Source: White River School District. Used with permission.

collaboratively focuses on results, shouldn't the central office develop such plans as well?

4. Most important, the plan must help us determine the degree to which we are affecting student learning in the White River School District.

BACKGROUND AND SOURCES OF DATA

The first step in our assessment plan was the collection of data that enabled us to determine where we were on our journey—our current reality. For White River, our plan focused primarily on four sources of data, both measurable (quantitative) and nonmeasurable (qualitative). It may be helpful to think of each of the data sources as a leg on a four-legged stool. Each leg, by itself, provides limited insight to our current reality. However, an analysis and synthesis of data from all four sources will provide us with a much sharper picture.

(A) Leg One: Survey and Interview Data

Becoming a professional learning community is a complex and at times difficult endeavor, and it is unreasonable to think that everyone views everything the same way. On the other hand, perceptions are important. They affect how we act and how we feel. The White River assessment of progress used survey data to determine perceptions of various groups regarding the *individual components* of the professional learning community concept—components such as the foundation of a PLC (mission, vision, values, and goals), the critical questions of learning, collaborative teaming, and a focus on results. Faculty and administrators participated in the survey. The results of this survey allowed us to target specific questions and groups for follow-up, in-depth, semistructured interviews. This combination of a broadly administered survey followed by focused, in-depth interviews enabled us to get a general view of how various groups view our progress in specific areas.

(B) Leg Two: Anecdotal Evidence

Remember some of the journeys you have taken with family or friends? Remember the stories you tell about things you remember—some good and some not so good? While such stories cannot be measured in a statistical sense, they are nevertheless important and powerful indicators of our current reality. In-depth, semistructured interviews were conducted with representatives from various groups. A structured part of the interview was developed based on an analysis of survey results. These were questions that needed more elaboration than could be gleaned from a survey alone. Additionally, part of the interview was open ended, when participants were encouraged to elaborate on any aspect of White River's PLC journey. While a single comment may not be significant, *patterns* of comments can be strong indicators of where we are as a district.

In addition to the interviews, a learning session specifically focused on assessing our progress on the journey to becoming a professional learning community was held with the White River Board of Directors. Certificated staff members from every level, staff members representing the views of beginning teachers, and a classified staff member responded to the following two questions:

1. How has doing your work as a professional learning community affected you professionally?

2. How has doing your work as a professional learning community affected student learning in your classroom and on your team?

(C) Leg Three: Products and Artifacts

In order to determine what we have done, what we have accomplished, and more important, the *quality* of our work, products and artifacts that have been produced by both faculty and administration were examined against a set of predetermined standards of quality. Examples of products and artifacts that were examined included team norms; school vision and commitment statements; power standards for each subject, grade level, and course; common pacing guides; collaboratively developed common assessments; and plans to provide students with additional time, support, and enrichment.

An analysis of these documents enabled us to establish improvement goals for not only the district and schools but individual teams. Like students, teams learn at different rates and in different ways, and just as in a classroom where differentiated instruction is emphasized, an analysis of team products and artifacts is enabling us to differentiate our approaches to improving the quality of the work that is done in each school and individual teams.

(D) Leg Four: Student Achievement Data

With the emphasis that is placed on the professional learning community concept within the White River School District, it would be easy to conclude that our mission is to become a professional learning community. We *do* seek to function as a truly effective professional learning community, but the PLC framework is simply a vehicle to enable us to achieve our mission of high levels of learning for all students—and adults. Thus, an analysis of districtwide achievement patterns was an essential component of our assessment plan. *This did not require additional testing, but rather a meta-analysis of existing data patterns.*

ADDING MEANING TO THE DATA

Data collection was simply the first step of assessing our progress on the journey to becoming a professional learning community. We recognized that data alone would not *inform* us. The critical component of the White River plan was determining what the data *meant*. This involved identifying patterns, asking questions, understanding perceptions, and gaining valuable insights. In short, not only is this report data driven, ultimately, its value lies in the *meaning* that is derived from it and its use as the basis for our district and school learning improvement plans and future decision making.

ANALYSIS OF DATA FOR DECISION MAKING

The ultimate purpose of our assessment plan is to help us *make better decisions*. Otherwise, we will simply be guessing what we should do next. Thus, the analysis of our data will enable us to make more informed decisions in the following areas.

(A) Determining Focus Areas for Next Steps on Our PLC Journey

Of course, once we have a clear understanding of where we are—our current reality—we must ask the next question: Where are we going next? A thorough assessment of our progress thus far enables us to set realistic and attainable goals for the future. Clear, concise goals, frequently referred to and monitored, will help us know exactly where we are trying to go next in achieving our mission of enhancing student learning.

(B) Structural Analysis

What changes need to be considered in our structure that will enable us to function more effectively as a professional learning community? Structure can be defined as policies, procedures, rules, organizational charts, role definitions, and so on. We want to ensure that our policies and our formal organizational structure are compatible with our desire to function as a high-performing professional learning community and thus enable more students to learn more. It's been said that when an organization begins to function as a professional learning community, everything changes. For example, do we need to re-examine our administrator evaluation program, our teacher observation format, and our overall teacher evaluation program? The professional development plans? Our hiring process? The way we allocate resources? Our organizational chart? These are but a few of the structural issues that we will analyze as a result of this report. We are constantly asking, "Does our structure reflect what we say we value?"

(C) Cultural Analysis (Our Day-to-Day Operation)

We cannot simply organize ourselves into a professional learning community. While changing our structure may be necessary, by itself it will be woefully inadequate. Ultimately, we must affect our culture—the collective beliefs, assumptions, values, and habits that represent the norm of the White River School District. Culture can be described as the way we do things around here. For example, what signals do we send about what we really care about? What trumps learning? What behaviors do we model? What do we check on? What are we willing to confront? What do we celebrate? What questions are we struggling to answer? What messages are we constantly and consistently sending? Do we do things in a timely and efficient manner? What is the focus of our meetings? Do we have too many meetings? Are they efficient, and do they serve a purpose? Are we all on the same page, going in the same direction? Do we require unnecessary paperwork? Is there additional paperwork that is needed? Ultimately, functioning as a high-performing professional learning community involves affecting the *culture as well as the structure* of our school district.

(D) Monitoring Our Results

Just like an effective plan for assessing student learning, our plan for assessing our progress is both formative and summative. We are developing specific practices and procedures for frequently monitoring our progress along the way to make informed adjustments in our route, and annually determining how we did, where we are, and where we are going next. In other words, the White River plan for assessing our progress is cyclical. Thus, one important value of these 2008 data is the establishment of a baseline for comparison of future progress.

SUMMARY CONCLUSIONS: 2006–2008

The following conclusions have been gained after thorough analysis of survey data, in-depth interviews, examination of products and artifacts, and an analysis of student learning data.

(A) Survey Results

In the spring of 2008, a fifty-four-item survey was administered to all teachers and administrators in the White River School District. Results were statistically analyzed and disaggregated by total responses, all teachers, all administrators, all specialists, school, and school level (elementary, middle, and high school). The survey data revealed that the White River School District has made significant progress in the implementation of professional learning community concepts and practices. Ninety percent or more of the respondents agreed or strongly agreed that the mission of ensuring high levels of learning for all students has been clearly articulated and is understood throughout the district, with 85 percent feeling that the learning mission has become embedded in the district's culture.

Over 80 percent of the respondents report that the district's vision has been articulated and is reflected in the district's organizational structure and practices. The data do reflect the need for some individual schools to revisit their vision statement and more clearly describe the school they seek to become in order to achieve the mission of high levels of learning for all students and communicate this vision throughout the faculty. Approximately 20 percent of teacher respondents perceived that this had not been accomplished in their school. [Individual school data were attached.]

Analysis revealed the need to revisit the issue of the district and each school's development and articulation of the core values and commitments. Districtwide, over 80 percent felt this had been accomplished. However, data from individual schools indicate that some schools are further along than others in this aspect of building the foundation of a professional learning community. Also, approximately 27 percent of the respondents perceived that there was no specific plan for monitoring goals. Approximately 18 percent felt that decisions had not been made or reviewed in light of their impact on learning.

Collaborative teams are at the core of a school and school district that function as a professional learning community. Survey data indicate that the district has made significant progress embedding the collaborative team concept throughout the district. However, two areas stand out as needing additional focus. Almost one-fourth of the respondents felt that teams were not engaged in seeking out best practices, and approximately 30 percent felt that the issue of sequencing course/subject content and the development of common pacing guides had not been addressed. Since these data vary from school to school, the district has the ability to focus specifically where attention is needed. Additionally, over half of the respondents (53 percent) indicated that they did not feel they received frequent and timely data regarding their effectiveness in comparison to others. Of course, these data are influenced by the fact that a number of teams have not developed or properly utilized common formative assessments.

Overall, the data regarding collaborative teaming is overwhelmingly positive. By far, most respondents answered affirmatively on all but a very few questions. The point is the data will allow focused intervention by team and by school to improve in specific areas of what teams in a professional learning community do.

One particular area of the survey requires immediate attention—the area of what teams actually do. Thirty-one percent of the respondents did not perceive that teams had developed common assessments. Thirty-six percent of the respondents felt teams had not established proficiency levels for various standards, and 33 percent felt teams had not agreed to criteria for judging the quality of student work or applying these criteria to ensure consistency. Of particular significance was the fact that almost half (44 percent) of the respondents did not perceive that a schoolwide plan had been developed to provide additional time and support to students when they experience difficulty in their learning. And 43 percent did not believe a plan had been developed to provide for enrichment when students reached a level of proficiency.

Of course, professional development is important in any school, but it is of particular importance in a professional *learning* community. On all items but one, respondents were overwhelming positive regarding training and professional development. However, over one-fourth of the respondents did not feel that student learning data were used to identify professional development needs.

The data reveal an additional area that needs attention—the area of planned recognition and celebration. Almost half (43 percent) did not feel there was frequent and public recognition and celebration for improvement in student learning.

As mentioned previously, on some specific items there were significant differences in responses between schools. Statistical analysis also revealed significant differences between administrator and teacher responses on a few survey items.

A statistical technique, chi-square analysis, was conducted to determine if distributions of scores across the various responses (strongly agree, agree, and so on.) were random or chance. The results indicate that the distribution of responses was not random and not equal, thus indicating significant differences for each of the questions in the percentage of respondents in each category. In other words, the results of this survey are statistically significant rather than simply chance.

An additional analysis was conducted to determine differences of perceptions between two categories of respondents—administrators and teachers—on each question. In general, administrators and teachers have comparable rates of agreement on most questions. However, there were differences of perception with administrators on some questions. These questions generally dealt with such areas as embedding the learning mission, goal setting, teams identifying criteria to judge the quality of student work, and developing systematic plans to provide students with additional time and support when they experience difficulty in their learning (questions 5, 13, 14, 19, 24, 31, 32, 36, and 37). In areas where significant differences between administrator perceptions and teacher perceptions were identified, administrator perceptions were higher or more favorable than those of teachers.

(B) Interview Analysis

The quantitative data from the survey provided the initial information regarding White River's progress toward functioning as a professional learning community and our impact on student achievement. However, quantitative data alone provide limited information. In order to gain a deeper, richer understanding of the impact professional learning concepts are having on district culture, follow-up interviews were conducted with teachers from across the district.

The interviews were specifically designed to gather qualitative data concerning the degree to which faculty have embraced and implemented the concepts and practices that form the framework of a professional learning community culture. Cultural change is a difficult, complex, and incremental endeavor that normally is initiated by the administration. However, to ultimately become a professional learning community, motivation must shift from one of *compliance* to one of *commitment*—from initial *externally* driven direction to a more *internally* driven purpose. In other words, cultural change most frequently goes through a process from knowing, to doing, to reflecting, to ultimately believing we can make a tremendous impact on the learning of every student.

The interviews were semistructured in nature. After answering a few standard, specific questions, teachers were encouraged to express their thoughts on a wide range of issues and ideas. Analysis of the interviews revealed a number of patterns.

Interview patterns indicated a very high degree of commitment to collaborative teaming in the White River School District. The following comments are typical:

- "Not having a PLC and having a PLC is night and day. I used to be so nervous and stressed. The goal was—survival. I would ask myself . . . can I get up and do this again? This English department PLC has made an amazing difference for me . . . my knowledge of the curriculum . . . my learning expectations for the kids."

- "For most of my thirty-plus year career, I felt like I was teaching in the wonder years. Like I wonder what that teacher is doing to get those results with her kids. Now we bring our results to the table, share instructional strategies, and are truly taking responsibility for the learning of all kids."

- "We now have a seventh-grade language arts teacher from Glacier who is part of our team. She is constantly telling us how much she is learning. She is now really questioning what she is doing daily in her classroom and stepping out a bit from her own interdisciplinary team. Having her on our team has helped us as well. She has a lot of questions, and we really have to think through her questions. We have to be clear on what we believe in . . . and why before we can answer her."

- "To some degree I have always had a partner to collaborate with, but it happened in the hallway or on the phone at night. Now we have directed time—it's intentional—we know what we want and need to do."

- "This PLC work has been great. I come together with another educator . . . the time is built in . . . there's a plan, and the best part is this . . . you are not alone making huge decisions about a child's learning."

- "This gift of time has really empowered me."

- "The best part for me . . . I get to collaborate and get help. And I can go to the share drive and just hit 'click,' and help is also right there! The mantra in the English department at our Monday PLC meetings is, I like that idea! Can I have that by first period?"

Teachers are genuinely excited about the district's commitment to and focus on high levels of learning for all students. For example:

- "For the first time the I-Search paper—well, every single piece/expectation of the paper is aligned. It doesn't matter which teacher is teaching it. Expectations are the same."

- "AP English and honors English are now working together."

- "We have worked together to make grading changes. For example, kids are now allowed to move from a 2 to 3 on the rubric if they improve the quality of their work. As a team we are not closing the door on learning for our kids."

- "I feel so much more accountable for teaching, evaluating results, and sharing the results. And more accountable for student learning."

- "This PLC process caused me to step up my teaching. I really want to be a better stronger teacher so more kids can learn more."

- "In the past as a grade 6–8 team, we would get together to align our scope and sequence, but some of us would get very frustrated because some staff would be teaching their favorite unit for a month and a half, and it wasn't even tied to the GLEs. Now with the top-down direction for our collaboration time, it's not okay to be teaching your favorite unit. The team holds you accountable to be teaching what you are supposed to be teaching. There is now a much greater focus on the GLEs and a better understanding of the GLEs. Kids are learning more of what they need to know versus what the teacher likes to teach."

- "Bringing data to the PLC has really impacted student learning. Often my data would show lots of kids that didn't meet the standard. Before I might go back and teach the same information a bit slower—hope they would get it—and then put the grades in the grade book. Now I get to brainstorm ideas with my team and discuss instructional strategies that I can try back in the classroom. Now guess what—after I reteach and bring the data back to the team—more kids got it!"

Of course, cultural change is influenced by structural changes. A number of teachers remarked that they appreciated the fact that the processes and procedures put into place have led to clearer communications and a greater sense of focus and organization throughout the district. These comments are typical:

- "I am one year from retirement and this is the best work I've done in my entire career."

- "This PLC work has now become so normal—working on curriculum . . . grading . . . creating rubrics . . . and common writing prompts . . . for the first time I wasn't alone. I am a better writing teacher because of the PLC."

- "The sharing of ideas at the cross-district grade-level meetings have been really helpful . . . I feel so supported! We get to problem solve together."

Some comments indicated a desire for the district to address specific areas. For example:

- "My grading has changed as well—we are through looking for top-down direction with this as well. I have eliminated the power of zero, and my gradebook reflects the standards versus a list of assignments."

- "The district needs to engage faculty and staff in developing a more comprehensive grading program. One that makes it easier to reflect the standards, set proficiency levels easily . . . et cetera. Teachers are trying to make these grading changes work in the current system, but it is a struggle."

- "At the middle level we also need more opportunities to look at student work like the elementary schools."

In summary, the patterns of comments from the interviews indicate that the district has made significant progress in moving the culture from one of compliance (top down) to commitment (bottom up).

The cultural shifts that are occurring in White River are indeed impressive. In addition to the qualitative data derived from interviews that are summarized here, impressions of White River's journey to become a truly functioning professional learning community have been captured on a brief video, which is included in this report.

(C) Product and Artifact Analysis

The journey to becoming a professional learning community requires teachers and administrators to develop a number of products. For example, schools must engage faculty and staff in the development of shared mission, vision, and value/commitment statements. Teams must develop norms and common assessments. Schools must develop a systematic plan to provide students with additional time, support, and enrichment. They must have plans to recognize and celebrate behaviors that represent the best examples of the school's vision and values/commitments, as well as improvement in student learning. Teams, for example, write team norms, identify and articulate power standards, write common assessments, and set SMART goals.

To determine the degree to which these products have been developed, as well as the quality of the products, samples were analyzed. Generally this review revealed that the development of products is uneven across the district. This was not unexpected, considering the fact that adults, like students, learn at different rates. For example, some teams have yet to write and utilize team norms. In every school, there are teams that are further along in the writing and use of common assessments, and few schools have a written plan for providing students with additional time, support, and enrichment. Less work has been done on the development of plans to recognize and celebrate learning improvement. And the quality of the products is also uneven. Attention will be paid to developing collaboratively agreed-upon standards of quality and assessing school and team products against these agreed-upon standards.

(D) Student Learning Data

As important as survey data and anecdotal evidence can be, the central question is this: How have our efforts to become a professional learning community affected student achievement? The answer is clear. In the White River School District, there are more students learning more than ever before.

Most important, more students passed the WASL in to 2008 than in 2007, and students in the White River School District performed at a higher level than the Washington State average. Of the twenty possible combinations of grade and content areas (for example, third-grade math), WRSD noted increases from the previous year on 75 percent of the combinations. This is in contrast to the results statewide. On the same combinations of grade and content areas, the state was at 55 percent.

Increases were noted in math for grades 3, 4, 5, and 6. Increases were noted in reading for grades 5, 6, and 8. Increases were noted for science in grades 5 and 8. Increases were noted for writing in grades 4, 7, and 10.

As encouraging as these data are, there is work to be done. The disaggregation of these data is allowing us to focus our improvement initiatives on specific schools, grade levels, subjects, and students.

In general, student achievement results are very encouraging and provide evidence of progress toward the district's mission of promoting high rates of learning for all students. However, there is much work to be done. As long as one student in the White River School District is struggling, we will not be satisfied. On the other hand, while there is work ahead, the evidence that the White River School District is making significant progress in the area of student achievement is clear, and there is much to celebrate.

PROFESSIONAL LEARNING COMMUNITIES AREAS OF FOCUS: 2008–2010

Based on a thorough analysis of data from the four sources described previously, the teaching and learning team will place an intense focus on the following areas during 2008–2009.

1. Standards of quality will be collaboratively developed for products that are expected from the district level, school level, and individual teams.

2. School mission, vision, and value/commitment statements will be reviewed and, where needed, revised.

3. Each school will develop a plan to monitor the work of individual teams.

4. Staff development will be provided to improve the quality of the work of teams.

5. Team common formative assessments will be reviewed and improved.

6. Each school will develop a plan to provide students who are experiencing difficulty in their learning additional time and support within the school day.

Plans to provide enrichment will be developed for students who demonstrate proficiency.

7. Plans will be developed at the district, school, team, and classroom levels to recognize and celebrate improvement—in both academic and nonacademic areas. Exemplary practices that best represent the district and school vision and values/commitments will also be recognized and celebrated. Celebrations will focus on the accomplishments of adults as well as students.

Specific plans will be developed to improve student achievement in specific courses, subjects, and grades in which students have not demonstrated sufficient academic gains.

Getting Started

We are frequently asked, "What resources would be particularly helpful when we begin implementing professional learning community concepts and practices?" Based on our work in White River and with other school district throughout North America, we have found the following resources to be particularly beneficial. (The full citation for each resource can be found in the references on page 213.)

When beginning the work of gaining shared knowledge of what a professional learning community is and how it works, we recommend that district leaders, principals, and at a minimum each team leader have a copy of DuFour, DuFour, Eaker, and Many's (2010) *Learning by Doing: A Handbook for Professional Learning Communities at Work* (second edition).

Realizing that many adults are visual learners, we recommend that the district office and each school have at their disposal at least one "roadmap"—Keating, Eaker, DuFour, and DuFour's (2008) *Journey to Becoming a Professional Learning Community.* The roadmap enables faculty and staff to determine where they are on their journey and to identify next steps that will need to be taken. It also serves as a way for everyone to see the big picture—how all the practices connect and support each other. The roadmap is particularly helpful since each stop on the map aligns with *Learning by Doing.* The vinyl hardcopy of the roadmap should be posted in a place where faculty and staff frequently gather to do their work and should be referred to frequently as professional learning community concepts and practices are being implemented.

District leaders and principals especially need to gain a deep, rich background in the professional learning community concept if they are to successfully lead the reculturing efforts in their district and schools. We recommend they read DuFour, DuFour, and Eaker's (2008) *Revisiting Professional Learning Communities at Work: New Insights for Improving Schools.* A deep understanding of professional learning community concepts and practices is enhanced by group discussion and reflection around the main sections of the book.

Teachers want to hear from other teachers. We recommend that the district purchase enough copies of the video series *The Power of Professional Learning Communities at Work: Bringing the Big Ideas to Life* (DuFour, Eaker, & DuFour, 2007) to enable each principal to view and discuss each video with his or her faculty.

As district leaders begin to build shared knowledge and build the foundational pieces of a professional learning community (shared mission, vision, values/commitments, and goals), we have found Marzano's (2003) *What Works in Schools: Translating Research Into Action* to be especially helpful. When faculty and staff engage in the collaborative process of describing the school they seek to become, they first need to gain an understanding of what effective schools are like—what they do and how they work. This book is an excellent resource.

One of the first tasks teams will tackle is clarifying and adding meaning to state and provincial standards, with a particular emphasis on identifying the most essential standards. *The Leader's Guide to Standards: A Blueprint for Educational Equity and Excellence* (Reeves, 2002) is particularly useful in explaining the importance of identifying power standards.

Each school will be directed to collaboratively develop a plan to provide students with additional time, support, or enrichment within the school day—regardless of the teacher to whom they are assigned. Two resources—Buffum, Mattos, and Weber's (2009) *Pyramid Response to Intervention: RTI, Professional Learning Communities, and How to Respond When Kids Don't Learn* and DuFour, DuFour, Eaker, and Karhanek's (2010) *Raising the Bar and Closing the Gap: Whatever It Takes*—are valuable for this work.

We have found two websites to be absolutely essential for doing the work associated with reculturing districts and schools into professional learning communities. We view www.allthingsplc.info and www.allthingsassessment.info as the 9-1-1 for those who are undertaking the PLC journey.

References

Ainsworth, L., & Viegut, D. (2006). *Common formative assessments: An essential part of the integrated whole.* Thousand Oaks, CA: Corwin Press.

allthingsplc. (n.d.). *Evidence of effectiveness.* Accessed at www.allthingsplc.info/evidence /evidence.php on May 15, 2011.

Berry, L., & Seltman, K. (2008). *Management lessons from the Mayo Clinic: Inside one of the world's most admired service organizations.* New York: McGraw Hill.

Buffum, A., Mattos, M., & Weber, C. (2009). *Pyramid response to intervention: RTI, professional learning communities, and how to respond when kids don't learn.* Bloomington, IN: Solution Tree Press.

Burns, J. M. (1978). *Leadership.* New York: Harper and Row.

Christman, J., Neild, R., Sullivan, K., Blanc, S., Liu, R., Mitchell, C., et al. (2009). *Making the most of interim assessment data: Lessons from Philadelphia.* Accessed at http://pdf.researchfroaction.org/rfapdf/publication/pdf_file/558/Christman_J _Making_the_Most_of_Interim_Assessment_Data.pdf on August 25, 2011.

Conzemius, A., & O'Neill, J. (2002). *The handbook for SMART school teams.* Bloomington, IN: Solution Tree Press.

Deal, T., & Kennedy, A. (1982). *Corporate cultures: The rites and rituals of corporate life.* Reading, MA: Addison-Wesley.

DuFour, R. (2002). *Passion and persistence: How to develop a professional learning community.* Bloomington, IN: Solution Tree Press.

DuFour, R., DuFour, R., & Eaker, R. (2004). *Let's talk about professional learning communities: Getting started.* Bloomington, IN: Solution Tree Press.

DuFour, R., DuFour, R., & Eaker, R. (2008). *Revisiting professional learning communities at work™: New insights for improving schools.* Bloomington, IN: Solution Tree Press.

DuFour, R., DuFour, R., Eaker, R., & Karhanek, G. (2004). *Whatever it takes: How professional learning communities respond when kids don't learn.* Bloomington, IN: Solution Tree Press.

DuFour, R., DuFour, R., Eaker, R., & Karhanek, G. (2010). *Raising the bar and closing the gap: Whatever it takes.* Bloomington, IN: Solution Tree Press.

DuFour, R., DuFour, R., Eaker, R., & Many, T. (2006). *Learning by doing: A handbook for professional learning communities at work.* Bloomington, IN: Solution Tree Press.

DuFour, R., DuFour, R., Eaker, R., & Many, T. (2010). *Learning by doing: A handbook for professional learning communities at work* (2nd ed.). Bloomington, IN: Solution Tree Press.

DuFour, R., & Eaker, R. (1998). *Professional learning communities at work: Best practices for enhancing student achievement.* Bloomington, IN: Solution Tree Press.

DuFour, R., Eaker, R., & DuFour, R. (Eds.). (2005). *On common ground: The power of professional learning communities.* Bloomington, IN: Solution Tree Press.

DuFour, R., Eaker, R., & DuFour, R. (2007). *The power of professional learning communities at work: Bringing the big ideas to life.* Bloomington, IN: Solution Tree Press.

Eaker, R., DuFour, R., & DuFour, R. (2002). *Getting started: Reculturing schools to become professional learning communities.* Bloomington, IN: Solution Tree Press.

Eaker, R., & Keating, J. (2008). A shift in school culture. *Journal of Staff Development, 29*(3), 14–17.

Eastwood, K., & Seashore Louis, K. (1992). Restructuring that lasts: Managing the performance dip. *Journal of School Leadership, 2*(2), 213–224.

Fullan, M. (2005). *Leadership and sustainability: System thinkers in action.* Thousand Oaks, CA: Corwin Press.

Handy, C. (1995). Managing the dream. In S. Chawala & J. Renesch (Eds.), *Learning organizations: Developing cultures for tomorrow's workplace* (pp. 45–56). New York: Productivity.

Hattie, J. (2009). *Visible learning: A synthesis of over 800 meta-analyses relating to student achievement.* New York: Routledge.

Keating, J., Eaker, R., DuFour, R., & DuFour, R. (2008). *The journey to becoming a professional learning community.* Bloomington, IN: Solution Tree Press.

Marzano, R. J. (2003). *What works in schools: Translating research into action.* Alexandria, VA: Association for Supervision and Curriculum Development.

Marzano, R. J., Pickering, D. J., & Pollock, J. I. (2004). *Classroom instruction that works: Research-based strategies for increasing student achievement.* Alexandria, VA: Association for Supervision and Curriculum Development.

Pfeffer, J., & Sutton, R. I. (2000). *The knowing-doing gap: How smart companies turn knowledge into action.* Boston: Harvard Business School.

Reeves, D. B. (2002). *The leader's guide to standards: A blueprint for educational equity and excellence.* San Francisco: Wiley.

Waters, T., & Marzano, R. (2006). *School district leadership that works: The effect of superintendent leadership on student achievement.* Denver, CO: Mid-continent Research for Education and Learning.

Index

A Leader's Companion
Inspiration for Professional Learning Communities at Work™
Robert Eaker, Rebecca DuFour, and Richard DuFour
Treat yourself to daily moments of reflection with inspirational quotes collected from a decade of work by renowned PLC experts. The uplifting wisdom inside this book will fuel your passion to be a leader in your PLC.
BKF227

The Journey to Becoming a Professional Learning Community
Janel Keating, Robert Eaker, Richard DuFour, and Rebecca DuFour
The Journey to Becoming a Professional Learning Community identifies key checkpoints for staying on track with deep implementation of PLC at Work™ concepts. Perfect for visual learners, the roadmap banner and accompanying booklet guide educators through critical issues that may arise during their journey.
BKF260

Learning by Doing
A Handbook for Professional Learning Communities at Work™
Richard DuFour, Rebecca DuFour, Robert Eaker, and Thomas Many
The second edition of *Learning by Doing* is an action guide for closing the knowing-doing gap and transforming schools into PLCs. It also includes seven major additions that equip educators with essential tools for confronting challenges.
BKF416

Revisiting Professional Learning Communities at Work™
New Insights for Improving Schools
Richard DuFour, Rebecca DuFour, and Robert Eaker
This tenth-anniversary sequel to the pivotal book *Professional Learning Communities at Work™* offers advanced insights on deep implementation, the commitment and consensus issue, and the human side of PLCs. Gain greater knowledge of common mistakes to avoid and new discoveries for success.
BKF252

Wait! Your professional development journey doesn't have to end with the last pages of this book.

We realize improving student learning doesn't happen overnight. And your school or district shouldn't be left to puzzle out all the details of this process alone.

No matter where you are on the journey, we're committed to helping you get to the next stage.

Take advantage of everything from **custom workshops** to **keynote presentations** and **interactive web and video conferencing**. We can even help you develop an action plan tailored to fit your specific needs.

Let's get the conversation started.

Call 888.763.9045 today.